WAYS
TO BE
THANKFUL

LISA M. GERRY

NATIONAL
GEOGRAPHIC
KiDS

WASHINGTON, D.C.

Being **thankful** means **paying attention and acknowledging** the things **going right in our lives** instead of dwelling on what's going wrong. It sounds simple, right? **And it is, really.**

But it's also **LIFE-CHANGING.**

Practicing gratitude is like putting on a pair of **what's good** goggles. **It's making the decision to look for all the little and big things that are awesome**—or even just A-OK—**throughout your day.**

By taking the time to notice and tune in to all the awesome things—like the taste of your morning muffin, the smell of honeysuckle on your walk to school, the incredible constellation of freckles on your face, your cat's cute little nose, or your best friend's laugh—you'll begin to see **even more awesome things start to happen.** It's like the **GOOD** starts to **MULTIPLY.**

When you make the decision to sit with those good gratitude feelings, **it can transform the way you feel on a daily basis.** Researchers have found that people who practice gratitude may notice a **lift in their mood, kinder feelings toward others, and a greater sense of peace.** Um, yes please!

Adopting an attitude of gratitude is like developing a **superpower.** While you might not be able to fly or see through brick buildings with x-ray vision, you will be able to find little bits of good sprinkled throughout the toughest of times. **This practice is a muscle and when you exercise it, you will become stronger and it will become easier.**

And research has found that **people who are thankful tend to do good stuff for other people, making other people's lives—and the world—better.** A recent study showed that when people do good stuff for other people, it actually changes their brains! **Gratitude is some powerful stuff!**

This book is filled with ways to strengthen those gratitude muscles. **There are crafts and projects, challenges and fun quizzes— all to help you notice and feel more thankful for the amazingness in your life.**

We all have the **power to focus on and appreciate the positive in our lives and in the world.** So, read on and get ready to be inspired, get **motivated,** and learn new ways to say—and give—thanks!

Oh, and **thank YOU**
for reading!

5

Make Time for
Belly Laughs.

Laughter is like joy bubbling out of your body. It's the song your soul sings when it's happy. Whether you've got a goofy giggle, a cheeky chortle, or a loud LOL, take a second to experience how good it feels to laugh. Then go ahead and laugh some more.

LAUGHING MATTERS

Not only does laughing *feel* great, it's actually healthy for you! Laughing decreases the stress hormones in your body, improves your immune system, and boosts endorphins, which are happy-making chemicals that your brain releases.

NEED A LITTLE INSPIRATION?
Check out these five
knee-slappers from Nat Geo's
Just Joking book series.

Q What do you call a sneezing train?

A Ah-choo-choo.

Q What is it called when two dinosaurs bump into each other?

A A Tyrannosaurus wreck.

Q What do you call a chicken staring at a head of lettuce?

A Chicken sees-a salad.

Q When do mice like to relax?

A The squeak-end.

Q Where do tigers exercise?

A Jungle gyms.

If you're in the market for more happiness (and who isn't?), this is for you. Gratitude is appreciation for what's good and meaningful to you in your life. Studies have found that thinking about things that you're grateful for can make you happier, help you sleep better, improve your health, benefit your relationships, ease aggression, raise your self-esteem, reduce stress, and more.

One **powerful way** to put gratitude into practice is by keeping a **GRATITUDE JOURNAL.**

STEP ONE. Throughout your day, be on the lookout for anything good. Pay attention to happy feelings, positive thoughts, fun, love, and laughter. All of these are sure to point you toward things to be thankful for.

STEP TWO. At the end of every day, write down three things that you're grateful for. Be specific.

You might be grateful for your **sweet grandma,** or that your cold finally went away. Perhaps you're grateful that your friend **saved you a seat on the bus,** or for the **warm, chewy brownie** you ate last night. You could be grateful for the **big oak tree** you pass on the way to school, or that you were voted class president. **Big, small,** and everything in between—**GRATITUDE comes in all shapes and sizes.**

3

Use Your IMAGINATION.

How cool is it that you can create any kind of world you want inside your head? There, you can be a brave astronaut befriending aliens, a powerful hero saving the world, or a fearless explorer on the hunt for lost treasures. The possibilities are endless! To show your appreciation for your amazing, magical mind, exercise your creativity like you would a muscle. Spend time every day letting your imagination run wild.

GIVE IT A >>GO!

Take out a piece of paper, choose one of these writing prompts, and for 10 minutes, write about **whatever** comes to mind. **The more wacky and wild the better!**

Writing Prompt 1:
Imagine you are on a walk in your neighborhood, when all of a sudden, you notice a little golden door on the sidewalk. This door has never been there before. It's much smaller than a regular door, but just big enough for you to squeeze through, and there is a bright light beaming through the cracks all around it. You walk over to the door and open it. Whoa! You can't believe your eyes. What do you see? What happens next?

Writing Prompt 2:
You've just won one million dollars in the lottery! How do you celebrate? How do you spend your money? How does your life change?

Writing Prompt 3:
Imagine you could choose any superpower for one day. What superpower would you choose? What would you spend the day doing? Where would you go? Who would you visit? What would be the top three things you'd want to experience using this superpower?

Appreciate All the **Amazing** Things Your **Body** Can Do.

4

It's **easy to get caught up** thinking about what your **body cannot do.** For instance, you might **not** be able to **slam-dunk,** you might **not** be able to **run a mile,** and hey, you still might **not** be **tall enough** to ride on that awesome new roller coaster with five full loop-the-loops. Your body might **not** be able to **spontaneously sprout the kind of hair you wish you had,** you might not be able to **sing a lick,** and you may be hopeless when it comes to **hula hooping.**

The truth is, there will **always, always** be things you **wish** your body could do **better, faster,** or even at all. But, if you spend your time thinking about those things, you will miss out on the chance to be **super-duper happy in the body you have.** So, whenever you start to think about the things you **can't do,** picture a **stop sign in your mind.** Then, switch to thinking about the things your **body can do.** Even when you're **feeling down** and it doesn't seem like your body can do much, **start small and make a list.**

Can you **walk** to the mailbox? Can you **bend down** to tie your shoes?

When your **favorite song** comes on the radio, can you **move your body** to the beat?

Can you hold **someone's hand** when they're scared? Can you give your mom and dad **a hug?**

Can you **feel** the sun or the wind or the rain **on your skin?**

If you answered **yes** to any of these, then your **body** is **already amazing.**

Take Care of Your Body.

Now that you've **made a list** of all the **amazing** things your **body can do** (#4), put your **appreciation** into action by keeping it **healthy** and **happy**.

1. **Get enough sleep.** Most doctors recommend that kids ages 6 to 12 should regularly get 9 to 12 hours a day for optimal health.

2. **Find ways to relax.** Stress can hurt your health, so find some ways to unwind, like reading a book, listening to music, meditating, walking, painting, or hanging out with friends.

3. **Exercise.** Experts also recommend kids and teens do 60 minutes or more of physical activity each day. That could be skateboarding, break dancing, playing soccer, or even pogo-sticking (uh, that's a word, right?). The important thing is to just get your body moving!

4. **Eat fruits and vegetables.** Try to eat fewer sweets and salty snacks and instead eat more things that grow from trees and sprout from the soil.

5. **Protect your noggin.** Wear a helmet when you ride your bike, skateboard, or roller skates.

6. **Wear your seatbelt.**

6

DO WHAT YOU CAN TO **MAKE** THE **WORLD** A **BETTER** PLACE.

CORINNE HINDES

When Corinne Hindes was 11 years old, she noticed a homeless man on the side of the road near where she lived in California, U.S.A. "He didn't have a single bag or a change of clothes," says Corinne. "All he had was a T-shirt and ratty, ripped up jeans." Instead of turning away or going on with her day, Corinne decided she wanted to do something to help. "I felt like I couldn't continue to look at him and not do anything. I was part of his community, and I had to help him. I finally turned to my mom and said, **'Mom, we *have* to do something.'"**

And do something she did. Corinne, who was an avid ski racer, spent a lot of time at ski resorts. During one of her frequent visits to the lost and found to find her runaway hat, she had an idea. **She could collect the bags of winter clothes left behind at ski resorts** (which previously were given to secondhand shops like Goodwill) **and donate them to homeless shelters.**

Six years later, Warm Winters has grown into a successful nonprofit. **"We're in 13 states now, 33 ski resorts, and we've helped more than 33,000 people,"** says Corinne. "It's been an amazing journey." And the man she saw on the side of the road? "His name is Billy," she says. "I was able to get clothes to him for many years. **He has a job now, an apartment, a car, and a dog. He's doing really well!"**

On the next page, Corinne talks about how she's making the world better by helping others. Read on to learn more, get inspired, then be on the lookout for opportunities for you to do good, too!

Q How did you know how to start a nonprofit when you were just 11 years old?

A When we first started, we would do it all ourselves: pick up the lost and found at the ski resort, load it into our car, take it home, sort through everything, and then take it either to the homeless shelter or pass items out face-to-face on the street. Then, in 2013, we partnered with The Jefferson Awards and got our official nonprofit status. My mother has been a great mentor to me. She's taught me so much about what it means to run an organization and a business.

Q What made you want to keep going and expand Warm Winters?

A Honestly, the gratification I got from passing out the clothes face-to-face kept me going. I would sit and talk to these people for hours. I would listen to their stories and make friends with them. So often, people living on the streets are ignored, and no one even looks at them. I could feel the joy they felt having someone show interest in what they had to say. It was the most powerful thing for me.

Q It sounds like the fact that you treated these people with dignity was as meaningful to them as the warm clothes you gave them.

A Absolutely. Something that I've learned is the value of face-to-face interaction. The number one thing that I encourage my volunteers to do is to go to the streets and talk with someone. [Note: We encourage our volunteers to have a buddy with them and always have a parent present if they are under 15.] These are people who aren't asked those questions—ones that we get asked on a daily basis—because people tend not to pay attention to them. Learn their name, find out where they were born. Ask how they got to the streets and what their passions are.

Q What's next for you?

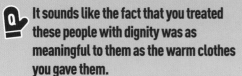

A I am headed to college to study business management and leadership, and will hopefully continue to grow Warm Winters. I want to continue to build a movement, create change, and help people.

Q What advice would you give other young people who want to make the world a better place?

A You can't change the whole world in a day, but you can take a small step to change one person's whole world in a day. It's the little things that really add up to create movements and help people. It can be something as simple as a conversation. Anything that you have to give is worth something, so nothing is too small.

Q How does being thankful play a role in doing good for other people?

A Taking care of the community, embracing the people around you, giving each other love and anything else that you can; it's just a healing process, and gratitude itself is a form of healing.

Q When do you feel grateful when you're working with Warm Winters?

A I feel most grateful when I'm talking to people who are homeless, when I'm able to hear their stories and have them confide in me. I'm most grateful in those moments, because someone who has never met me before suddenly has the trust in me to share a story and tell me a little bit about themselves. I think that is incredible.

TAKE GOOD CARE OF YOUR PETS!

7

Pets. Are. The. BEST! They're sweet snuggle monsters, super funny, and crazy cute, and they bring us so much happiness. The best way to show your pets you're thankful for them is to take great care of them. To do that, take them on walks, feed them healthy foods, brush them, give them a safe space to live and play, and take them for regular vet visits.

Stand by for cuteness!
Three *National Geographic Kids* readers
introduce us to their precious pets.

Henry, 14, and his dog, Maisy, 8

Maisy's Favorite Toy: Maisy's "baby" is an off-white, fleece star.

Maisy's Best Trick: Catching popcorn and treats in her mouth midair!

Henry's Favorite Thing About Maisy: Her kind personality and her fluffiness—she's so soft to pet!

Sayla, 15, and her dog, Max, 8

Max's Favorite Toy: His squeaky snowman.

The Cutest Thing About Max: His ears!!

Sayla's Favorite Thing About Max: No matter what emotion you're feeling, he's always there for you!

Teagan, 10, and her cat, Basil, 2

Basil's Favorite Toy:
Absolutely anything with a feather!

Basil's Best Trick:
He can jump up on surfaces on command.

Teagan's Favorite Thing to Do With Basil:
Taking him for walks outside on a leash. Basil will let anyone pick him up. He's very gentle and never uses his claws.

APPRECIATION STATION

If you're desperate for a dog, but one's not in the cards for you right now, don't worry—there are other ways to have a playdate with a pup. You can volunteer at a local animal shelter, and there are now apps, like Wag!, that will match a dog lover in need of some furry-friend time with someone who needs a dog walker—or even with a dog living in a shelter that needs to be walked. Of course, ask your parents first!

8

Show Your Family You LOVE THEM

(even though they sometimes drive you crazy!).

Sure, it's **embarrassing** when your mom licks her finger to get something off your cheek, and yes, it's **super annoying** when your brother puts his retainer on the side of his plate at dinner. But this **wild bunch is still your family,** and sometimes, they're even pretty great.

9

Take stock of what you **do** have.

Like a roof over your head.

There are two ways to compare— comparing UP or **comparing DOWN.**

Comparing UP

means that you are comparing YOURSELF, YOUR LIFE, or your CIRCUMSTANCES to someone who you THINK has it BETTER THAN YOU. For example, you might think, "My friend Beatrice has her own bedroom and her own bathroom. My house is tiny. I don't even have my own room!"

This type of comparison and thinking about WHAT YOU DON'T HAVE or what you have LESS OF often leads people to FEEL ANXIOUS AND SAD.

Comparing DOWN

means that you are looking at what you do have with the understanding that SO MANY people throughout the world HAVE MUCH LESS. So you might say, "Wow, there are people in this world who don't have homes of their own. Even though I share my bedroom, I am SO LUCKY to have a warm place to sleep at night with soft sheets and a comfy pillow."

This type of comparison, which includes COMPASSION FOR OTHER PEOPLE and their struggles, is a GREAT WAY TO PRACTICE GRATITUDE.

10

Have a Party for Pizza!

Sure, pizza is a big (and delicious) part of most parties, but why not switch it up a bit and throw a party for pizza? If ever there was something to celebrate, it's pizza!

Five Fun Facts About Pizza:

1.
Pepperoni is the most popular topping in the United States and the United Kingdom.

2.
Pizza was invented in Naples, Italy, in the 1800s, when people began adding tomatoes to flat focaccia bread.

3.
Different countries like all sorts of different pizza toppings. In Japan, popular toppings include mayonnaise and squid. In Brazil, you might find green peas, raisins, or hardboiled eggs atop your pie.

4.
The average American is thought to eat about 23 pounds (10 kg) of pizza a year.

5.
The world record holder for largest pizza was made in Rome, Italy, in 2012 and had a total surface area of 13,580.28 square feet (1,261.65 m²). And bonus, it was gluten free!

PAY ATTENTION TO YOUR BREATH.

The **first step** to being thankful is **being present.** Being present helps you **stop** thinking about the past or **worrying about the future** so that you can **appreciate this very moment,** just as it is. Sometimes, it can be **hard** to be present when there's a lot going on inside your head. One way to **slooowww down** and center yourself in the here and now is to **pay attention to your breath.**

There are lots of **cool breathing exercises** you can try. Here are two to get you started.

SLOW DOWN, GET CENTERED, EXERCISE 1

1. Start by sitting or lying down in a comfortable place.
2. Place your right hand on your stomach and your left hand on your chest. As you breathe, notice the way your stomach and your chest rise and fall.

3. Close your mouth and gently breathe in through your nose for the count of four.
4. Hold your breath and count to three or four, whichever is most comfortable for you.
5. Then slowly exhale deeply through your mouth until it feels like no air remains in your lungs.
6. Repeat this five times, or until you feel calmer and more centered.

BREATHE YOUR WAY TO CALM, EXERCISE 2

1. Sit comfortably with your back straight and tall and your head held high.

2. Place the pointer and middle fingers of your right hand between your eyes.

3. Take a few gentle breaths.

4. Use your thumb to close your right nostril and inhale through your left nostril.

5. Use your ring finger to close your left nostril and hold your breath for three counts.

6. Open your right nostril and exhale slowly through it, then pause for a moment.

7. Inhale slowly through the right nostril now.

8. Close both nostrils and hold your breath for three counts.

9. Then open the left nostril and exhale slowly through it, pausing for a moment.

10. Now inhale slowly through the left nostril. Close both nostrils and hold your breath for three counts.

11. Repeat this cycle five to seven times, or until you feel calmer and more centered.

35

Be Aware of Your Impact on the Planet.

12

WHEN SOMETHING IS REALLY IMPORTANT TO YOU, IT MAKES SENSE THAT YOU WOULD WANT TO TAKE GOOD CARE OF IT, RIGHT?

Well, that same idea can be applied to more than just your new scooter or game console. Take, for instance, our oceans. Sure, oceans are crazy fun—you can snorkel in them, cruise in boats, and jump in their waves. And did you know that Earth's oceans are home to more than 700,000 species? And more than half of the oxygen we breathe comes from plants in the ocean. (It's produced as a by-product of photosynthesis by marine plants like plankton and kelp.)

So, yeah, oceans are pretty great.

Here are five ways you can help protect oceans:

1. Organize a beach cleanup with friends and family and spend a few hours picking up all of the trash you see.

2. Encourage your family to eat only sustainable seafood.

3. Recycle all plastic bags and bottles, because when thrown in the trash, they can end up in the ocean.

4. Learn about climate change and how not to contribute to it. Rising temperatures have a big impact on oceans, making the water warmer and more acidic, which disrupts the ecosystem.

5. When you're done building sandcastles and playing at the beach, fill in any holes so that newly hatched turtles heading to the ocean don't fall in (and then have trouble climbing back out).

Grace C. Young is an ocean engineer and a National Geographic Emerging Explorer. She recently spent 15 days living 66 feet (20 m) below the ocean in Aquarius, the world's only underwater laboratory. Aquarius, which is located off the Florida Keys, measures 43 x 20 x 16.5 feet (13 x 6 x 5 m) and weighs approximately 81 tons (74 t). It has six bunk beds, hot water, a mini-kitchen, climate control, computers, and wireless internet. Grace works to create technologies that help us better understand and manage the oceans. Right now, she builds cameras that help us see underwater in 3D. She uses them to study the ecosystem's health. So cool!

LOVE SOMETHING?

LEARN MORE
ABOUT ITS HISTORY!

Picture this: You strap on a cool helmet (maybe it has a unicorn horn or a faux spiky hairdo), put your schoolbooks in your basket, hop on your bike, and start peddling. The wind is on your face, your cheeks are flapping, and you ring your bell just because, why not? Right now, on this bike, life is good.

But did you know that bikes also have a really cool bikestory, er, backstory? Yep, that's right. Your precious peddler actually helped pave the way for women's rights.

When **BIKES** were invented in the 1800s, they were called **VELOCIPEDES.** Some had one giant front wheel, some had three or four wheels, and some didn't even have pedals (sort of like the balance bikes little kids ride today). But once bikes started catching on, **THEY WERE GAME CHANGERS.** In fact, at a time when women were expected to rely heavily on men, **BIKES GAVE THEM TREMENDOUS FREEDOM AND INDEPENDENCE.** Women **NO LONGER** had to wait for men to ready their horses; they could just hop on a bicycle and **HEAD OUT FOR A RIDE ON THEIR OWN.** For the first time ever, women could **GO WHERE THEY WANTED, WHEN THEY WANTED.** And it was **REVOLUTIONARY!**

WOMEN'S RIGHTS ACTIVIST AND SUFFRAGETTE SUSAN B. ANTHONY **SAID DURING THAT TIME,**

66 Let me tell you what I think of bicycling. I think it has done more to emancipate women than anything else in the world. 99

HONOR YOUR WILD IDEAS.

Sure, your ideas might be a little out-there, but many of the best ones are! Don't count 'em out just because they're kooky, and don't let naysayers discourage you from seeing your ideas through. Creativity requires that you think about things in new and interesting ways. Write down your ideas, share them with friends and family, come up with plans for how you could make your ideas a reality, and take a second to thank your brain for being so imaginative and unique.

43

15

Take Pleasure in *Little Things*

(no matter how weird).

Go ahead, be **delighted** in **little things** like brand-new school supplies, **bubble wrap,** folded chips, the smell of a library book, a **dog** with an **underbite,** pizza bubbles, or the sound of rain on the window.

catching **snowflakes** on your tongue

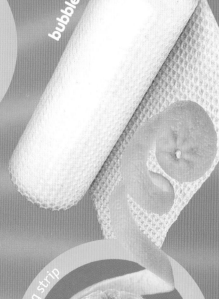

peeling a clementine in one long strip

bubble wrap

GIVE IT A
>> GO

Make a list of **five to 10 little things** that make **YOU** smile.

45

16 Marvel at RAINBOWS.

The word "marvel" means "to be filled with wonder and astonishment." Letting yourself be amazed by something is a great way to give thanks for things that might otherwise be taken for granted. Things like rainbows, for instance. Because, well, rainbows are awesome!

HOW DO RAINBOWS WORK?

You've probably already noticed that the prime time to spot a rainbow is when the sun begins to shine right after a rainstorm. That's because rainbows appear when light from the sun passes through raindrops. The light from the sun is called white light. And though it appears white to us, it is actually made up of seven different colors: RED, ORANGE, YELLOW, GREEN, BLUE, INDIGO, and VIOLET. But, when the white light passes through a raindrop, it scatters into the seven individual colors, which is called refraction. Then, the light—now separated into the seven different colors—bounces out of the raindrop, which is called reflection, making a rainbow!

APPRECIATION
★ STATION ★

When Ella Tryon was six years old, she was admitted to the hospital for a severe food allergy. To lift her spirits, she decided to color a picture of a rainbow, but soon found out that the hospital's playroom didn't have all the colors she needed. So, Ella started the nonprofit Help Me Color A Rainbow to make sure other kids in hospitals had access to their own boxes of crayons. Since then, she has donated more than 30,000 boxes of crayons to children's hospitals in the United States. Go, Ella, go!

47

17

Treasure Friends Who Just *Get* You.

They'll join in on your **silly dances, talk with you for hours** about the characters in your favorite books, and **laugh their heads off** at jokes only you guys understand. There's no explanation needed when you're together— you're like **peas in a pod.**

18

And Treasure Friends Who *Challenge* You.

They **encourage you** to think about things in new ways, **introduce you** to foods you've never tried, and **teach you stuff** you never knew you didn't know. These **mind-opening** buds help you **see new perspectives**, respect different opinions, and have a broader understanding of the world.

19 Thank
YOUR LUCKY STARS FOR
Cute Things.

A fluffy, roly-poly puppy. A baby panda. A tiny turtle. A sleepy sloth.

When we see adorable animals, both in pictures and IRL, our brains release a chemical that makes us feel happy, loving feelings. Sometimes, we feel such a rush of big feelings, we may even grit our teeth and feel like we want to squeeze something (ahem, cheek-pinching grandmas). There's even a term for it: CUTE AGGRESSION.

In the Filipino language Tagalog, the word "GIGIL" means just that. It's "an uncontrollable feeling, when one is overwhelmed by an emotion, typically used in reference to something cute such as a baby or a puppy."

The next time you see something *aww*-inducingly cute, remember to appreciate the warm, happy feelings it gives you.

Bring on the cute!

Want to up the cute quotient in your life? Ask a parent if you can check out an animal live cam. Some zoos, national parks, and animal rescue nonprofits have found a way to share the cute by setting up cameras that stream live video of adorable animals to viewers around the world. You can spend hours watching brown bears fish for salmon on the Katmai National Park and Preserve website, pandas rolling and munching leaves on the Smithsonian's National Zoo Panda Cam, or even the soothing sight of sea nettles swimming on the Vancouver Aquarium's Jelly Cam.

ERIKA
SKOGG

JUMP (20) at the chance to TRAVEL.

ERIKA SKOGG is a WORLD TRAVELER and a self-proclaimed TRAVEL LOVER! She teaches photography workshops and leads groups on National Geographic Expeditions in places like MOROCCO, CUBA, and THE GALÁPAGOS.

Q When did you discover your passion for travel?

A In college, I signed up for a study abroad semester in Italy to study photography. It was the first time I ever traveled alone, especially in a new country where I didn't speak the language. I was so nervous to leave home and do something by myself, but I quickly learned that it was incredibly easy to maneuver my way through Italy using trains and buses, by asking for help, and simply following the signs.

I had so much fun learning how to read guidebooks and exploring places all by myself, and from there I was inspired to spend an entire year in Taiwan teaching English. I spent the weekends traveling the country by scooter, and during my time in Asia, I even took a trip to Thailand and Cambodia by myself. I kept meeting friendly people from all over the world and never once ended up eating a meal alone.

55

JUMP AT THE CHANCE TO TRAVEL.

Q Why do you think travel can be such a transformative experience for people?

A Travel gives us the opportunity to meet people from other countries who have had different life experiences than us, and who, therefore, have different points of view. It's very easy to feel that the differences between "us" and "them" can be intimidating or scary, but travel allows us the opportunity to form ideas for ourselves, instead of listening to the news or other people's opinions.

Q How does gratitude play a role in your travels?

A I have always felt most grateful to the complete strangers who make my trips not only memorable but possible! I rely a lot on the people who live in the places I travel to help me find my way or allow me to take a photograph of them.

Also, traveling abroad has made me incredibly grateful for everything I was given growing up in the United States, which I wasn't truly aware of until I started traveling. I feel most grateful for the simple things now: access to clean water and a warm, comfortable place to sleep at night ... things I just assumed everyone else had as well.

Q What's one way that you like to express your gratitude?

A I like to print photographs I take of people during my travels. I either ask for their address so I can mail them a printed copy, or if I return to the country, I go out of my way to find them again and hand them back in person. Some people I give photos to have never had their photograph taken, let alone had a printed copy. Instead of just taking photographs, I like to give them back to say "Thank you."

Erika's **Top Five Reasons** to **Travel:**

1. Making incredible, lifelong friendships.
2. Practicing a new language so much I actually learn to speak it.
3. Getting away from screens (like phones!) and experiencing things in real life.
4. Learning I can be my own best friend, and sometimes needing to be.
5. It continues to give me exposure to many different lives all over the world, giving me tons of gratitude for my home, a place I admittedly have taken for granted in the past.

CURB THE
COMPLAINING.

Just like how exercising regularly makes it easier to run and jump and play, studies have found that by **THINKING NEGATIVE THOUGHTS REGULARLY,** you can actually **REWIRE YOUR BRAIN** in a way that makes negative thinking your default. Also, just being around people who complain a lot can really bring your mood and happiness level down. So, to keep yourself from becoming a **NEGATIVE NANCY** or a **DANNY DOWNER,** try not to dwell on things that you don't like and, instead, look on the bright side. **THEN PICK PALS WHO DO THE SAME.**

GIVE IT A >>GO!

Try not to complain for **one week.** Catch yourself when you do and switch gears to **find something going right.** So, sure, it might be raining and the bus might be late, but it's also **pizza day** at school and you're wearing a supercomfy new shirt. **TA-DA!**

You've **turned negative feelings** into **positive ones** all with the **power of your mind.**

22 THANK SOMEONE FROM YOUR PAST.

A quick way to boost positive feelings—both in you and someone else—is by **telling someone how much they mean to you.** One superspecial way to do this is by thinking of someone from your past who you may not have thanked way back when and **writing them a letter.**

Maybe it's someone who was **welcoming** when you started a new school, or a teacher who **made you feel better** when you were going through a hard time, or a soccer coach who stayed after practice **to teach** you how to juggle the ball.

Be specific, be sincere, and let them know how their actions made you feel. Then take a minute to think about how it would feel to receive a letter like that. Now pop it in the mail. You'll feel great and so will they!

23

Think of SOMETHING You're Looking FORWARD TO.

24

TURN UP the Music!

Music can **pump you up** when you need a boost, **keep you company when you're feeling glum,** and **give you all the feels** when you've got a crush. Here are five more reasons to give thanks to terrific tunes:

1. Playing a musical instrument has been found to **improve memory.**

2. Humans aren't the only ones who like to **dance—parrots** and **elephants** can get down and **boogie,** too!

MIN   MAX

4.
Musical instruments are works of art! Take the violin, for example. A single violin is made from more than **70 individual pieces of wood!**

3.
Music can help **calm you down** when you're nervous.

5.
Our brains release **happy-making chemicals** when we listen to music we like.

65

Be still. 25

When your **mind** is **busy** or things around you feel **chaotic,** it's very easy to get caught up and to forget what's really important. You may even feel nervous, overwhelmed, or **stressed out.** But, when you recognize that happening, there's something you can do. **You can slow down, get quiet, and BE STILL.**

25 BE STILL.

Turn off all your electronics and find a quiet place to sit or lie down.

If it helps you to listen to soft, soothing music, do that. Maybe you'd like to look at a **calming picture** from somewhere beautiful in nature—like a field of flowers or an underwater coral reef. Try watching the rain, leaves rustling on the trees, or birds **outside your window.**

Let yourself just be

still for a few minutes.

When your mind starts to drift to worries or things you need to do, **bring the focus back to your breath.**

GIVE IT A >> GO!

Do you need some stillness in your life but can't sit or lie down? No problem! Stillness and quiet are always within your reach. Even in the middle of a busy hallway or a crowded gym, you can stop, take a few deep breaths, and gently remind yourself to SLOW DOWN.

26

Think about the
BEST PART of your **day.**

Then share it with your family.

27 Marvel at SCIENCE.

Isn't science amazing? Through experimentation and observation, scientists are able to better understand the physical and natural worlds. Then they can apply what they've learned to invent new things to make our lives—and the world around us—better. Every once in a while, take a minute to think about, and appreciate, just how we benefit from the brainstorms and brilliance, discoveries and determination of scientists.

Turn the page for three scientific inventions to be super thankful for.

1. EYEGLASSES

The **FIRST EYEGLASSES** were invented in the **1200S IN ITALY.** They were worn by monks and scholars and either held up in front of their faces or balanced on their noses. After the printing press was invented in the **1400S, AND MORE PEOPLE BEGAN LEARNING TO READ,** the demand for glasses grew. Today, it's estimated that **75 PERCENT OF ADULTS IN THE UNITED STATES** use either glasses or contacts.

Ask an adult to help you look up organizations like the Lions Club (Lionsclubs.org) where you can donate your old eyeglasses to people in need.

2. PENICILLIN

Before the discovery of penicillin, doctors didn't have a way to fight patients' infectious diseases. **PEOPLE DIED** from what are now completely **CURABLE DISEASES,** like strep throat, and wounded soldiers often died from **INFECTION** rather than from their wounds. **IN 1928,** Alexander Fleming found some **MOLD GROWING IN AN UNCOVERED PETRI DISH** that contained *staphylococcal* bacteria. When he examined the Petri dish under a microscope, he saw that the bacteria close to the mold were **DYING!** Fleming was able to then identify the mold and, upon further inspection, he realized that it was the "juice" from the mold that was killing the bacteria. He called his **DISEASE-FIGHTING MOLD JUICE** "penicillin." **TODAY,** we still use penicillin to treat bacterial infections like ear and sinus infections.

3. WI-FI

It's hard to imagine life without WIRELESS COMMUNICATION. It's such an IMPORTANT part of how we send and receive information now. The SCIENCE BEHIND IT can be traced back to an invention by Hollywood actress Hedy Lamarr and her friend, composer George Antheil, who in the 1940s invented a SECRET COMMUNICATION SYSTEM to fight the Nazis in World War II. By switching radio frequencies in a preprogrammed pattern, their technology made it possible for CLASSIFIED MESSAGES to be sent by the government WITHOUT BEING INTERCEPTED by the enemy.

28

Follow Your CURIOSITY.

CURIOSITY is the desire to want to know or learn more about something. **INVESTIGATING** something you're interested in—whether it be comedy, cooking, or the cosmos—is a **GREAT WAY TO PUT YOUR APPRECIATION FOR IT INTO ACTION. RESEARCH, READ, TRY NEW THINGS, ASK LOTS OF QUESTIONS,** and **HAVE AN OPEN MIND.** Enjoy the process of **DISCOVERING** more about the things you find **FASCINATING.**

29

LEARN to

SAVOR.

Sometimes happy moments can feel like they're over in a flash. Savoring is a way to make the most out of happy, good feelings and make those feelings last longer. Here's how to let the good times grow:

PAY ATTENTION. One way to savor is to be present and to recognize the positive feelings you're experiencing in the moment. For example, if you're about to eat a delicious cookie, instead of gobbling it, Cookie Monster—style, slow down as you're eating it. Don't rush through your treat, give yourself plenty of time to make the most of it. Put away your phone, turn off the TV, and appreciate each bite that you take, paying close attention to all of the delicious flavors that you're tasting.

REMINISCE. Even though your vacation is over, your happy feelings about it don't have to be. Tell people about your fun adventures, share stories with people who were there, look through pictures and videos you took of your trip, and let your happy thoughts linger.

PASS IT ON. A great way to pump up positive feelings about something you love is to share it. Then, not only do you get to experience it, you'll feel great helping someone else experience it, too! So, the next time you hear a funny joke, tell other people! Or, if you read the best book, let a friend borrow it, so you can talk about it together. If you learn a new skill, teach someone else! If you discover a cool new candy, split some with a friend.

EXCHANGE
INFORMATIO
ACCOMMODAT
EXCURSIO
OUVENIRS / P
CHANG
TOP RATE

30 MAKE A GRATITUDE PLEDGE.

Gratitude, or being thankful for what's good in your life, is a mind-set. And it's a choice. You have to choose to look at all that's going right instead of dwelling on what's wrong.

GIVE IT A >>GO!

Write a **gratitude pledge** on a piece of paper, tape it somewhere that you'll **see it every day** (like your bathroom mirror), **and recite it to yourself each morning.** This pledge will serve as a **great reminder** to notice warm feelings, as well as **situations to be thankful for.**

Your pledge could be something like **"I pledge to notice good things,"** or **"I pledge to count my blessings,"** or **"I pledge to look on the bright side when things aren't going my way."**

31 GET COZY

There is nothing better than feeling warm and relaxed, so and snuggly. There is even a Danish word, *hygge* (pronou hoo-guh), that means the happiness and feeling of well-b that comes from simple, cozy pleasures.

Some things that might enhance the hygge in your life in thick, warm socks ... drinking hot chocolate while watchir snow fall ... lighting candles to create a soft glow ... a big comfy sweater ... a crackling fire in the fireplace ... throw blankets ... even your favorite pair of sweatpants (which Danes call *hyygebuskers*). Practicing hygge means findin great joy and comfort in small, simple pleasures.

GIVE IT A >> GO!

Make a list of five things that bring **hygge** into your life.

32

Smile.

When something GOOD happens, SMILING is one of the ways your body says "THANK YOU." And, even if YOU DON'T FEEL LIKE SMILING at anyone, just SMILING BY YOURSELF CAN HAVE SOME RADICAL RIPPLE EFFECTS. When you smile, chemicals like dopamine, endorphins, and serotonin are released in your brain. These help you RELAX, make you FEEL HAPPIER, and can even LOWER YOUR BLOOD PRESSURE AND DECREASE PAIN.

Now that's something to smile about.

"Sometimes your joy is the source of your smile, but sometimes your smile can be the source of your joy."
—Thich Nhat Hanh, spiritual leader and peace activist

33

TREASURE AWESOME TEACHERS.

Oh, what a difference a great teacher makes! Great teachers make learning fun, happily go the extra mile to make sure you understand, and make their students feel special. If you have a great teacher (or you've had one in the past), let them know!

"Let us *REMEMBER:* One **BOOK,** one pen, *ONE CHILD,* and **one teacher** can **change** the **world."**

—Malala Yousafzai, activist

(see page 193)

34 GO ON ADVENTURES.

Imagine flying in a helicopter along the coastline of Hawaii with your two best friends. To your right are majestic, mossy green sea cliffs and below you, there's nothing but a thousand feet of air and then the Pacific Ocean. Your mission today? To find a rare plant species on a remote island.

Pretty cool, right?

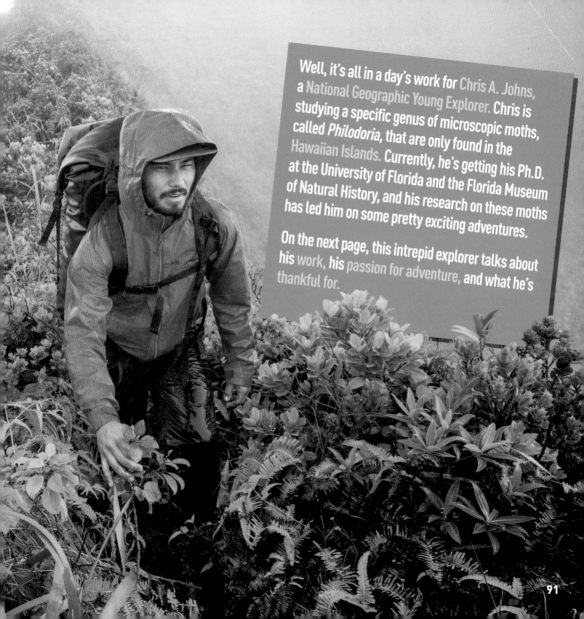

Well, it's all in a day's work for Chris A. Johns, a National Geographic Young Explorer. Chris is studying a specific genus of microscopic moths, called *Philodoria*, that are only found in the Hawaiian Islands. Currently, he's getting his Ph.D. at the University of Florida and the Florida Museum of Natural History, and his research on these moths has led him on some pretty exciting adventures.

On the next page, this intrepid explorer talks about his work, his passion for adventure, and what he's thankful for.

34 GO ON ADVENTURES.

Q HOW DID YOU DECIDE THIS IS SOMETHING YOU WANTED TO DO?

A I started doing environmental conservation work because I wanted to be outside. It was pretty simple: I like being outside with my friends. But over the course of training to be a scientist, I gained a much deeper appreciation of the natural world.

Q SO, HOW WOULD YOU DEFINE ADVENTURE?

A I would say that adventure is exploring something unknown. Personally, I like adventure when it's about 30 to 40 percent uncomfortable, and when it's with my good friends. I think adventures help you to continue developing who you are and your understanding of your place in the world.

Q HOW DOES ADVENTURE PLAY A ROLE IN THE WORK THAT YOU DO?

A It's all been an adventure. As of about 40 years ago, only two people had ever worked on this genus of micromoths, and only a handful of people even knew about them. So, the entire process of discovering more about this organism and exploring its biology has been an adventure in itself. I came into this project not knowing anything about insects, and now, I'm, like, the world expert on this one very tiny little moth.

Q WHAT IS ONE OF YOUR FAVORITE ADVENTURES THAT YOU'VE BEEN ON?

A My favorite field excursion for this project was to some cliffsides on the island of Molokai in Hawaii. They're some of the tallest sea cliffs in the world. Some of the best natural ecosystems often occur in these really steep areas, because the pigs and deer and goats that like to eat the native plants can't get to them. We wanted to go there to look for this super-rare, critically endangered plant that is in the sunflower family. The moth that I study specializes a lot on members of the sunflower family. So, two of my best friends and I got in a helicopter early one morning and flew along, right next to the sea cliffs. The helicopter pilot just put the very front of the skids down on the side of the cliff, and we delicately crawled out. We spent two days looking for the plant, and we actually found it! It hadn't been seen on that island for 30 years. We think we may have seen signs of a micromoth, *and* we also found a snail species that hadn't been seen in more than 50 years, which is pretty crazy.

Q WHAT ARE YOUR ADVENTURE MUST-HAVES?

A My tent, my sleeping mat, a rain jacket, a long-sleeve shirt, a headlamp, and I always end up bringing far more camera gear than I need.

A They're about the size of a small eyelash in length and width. They have these beautiful, long antennae that stretch back the whole length of their body. The coolest part, I think, is that they have these crazy color patterns of oranges, blues, and these metallic, silvery colors spaced in between. If you were to see one on your finger, you wouldn't be able to tell, but once you look at them up close, they're pretty crazy looking.

Q *HOW DO YOU THINK BEING THANKFUL PLAYS A ROLE IN THE ADVENTURES THAT YOU GO ON?*

A The nice thing about being a biologist is that everyone in this field agrees that we don't know everything. It's wonderful. So, through adventure, through the research that a biologist does, through exploring the unknown, I get a better sense of where I fit into the entire picture—it's definitely something that I end up feeling grateful for all the time.

Q *HOW DO YOU LIKE TO EXPRESS YOUR GRATITUDE?*

A I like passing it on to other people. Gratitude is a really powerful tool to feel within yourself and to exercise in the world. I think it often gets expressed by being nice to other human beings and giving them the space and time to be who they are, and reflecting good things back to them.

35

CELEBRATE ALL THE WAYS YOU'RE UniQuE!

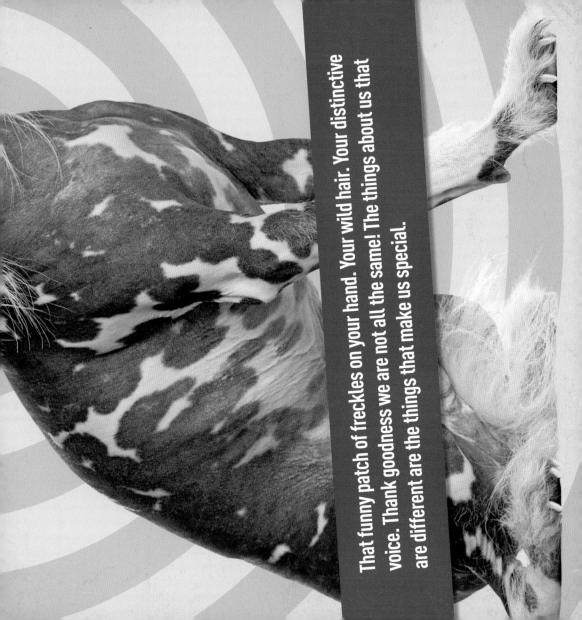

That funny patch of freckles on your hand. Your wild hair. Your distinctive voice. Thank goodness we are not all the same! The things about us that are different are the things that make us special.

36

Look UP and Admire the Sky.

When you're **RUSHING** to get to practice, **WAITING** at the bus stop, or **LOOKING DOWN** at a book or a game, you might not notice what's right above you. But today, **STOP WHAT YOU'RE DOING AND LOOK UP.** Do you see a butterfly? Clouds? Planes? Where you live, do you see just a sliver of the sky peeking out between buildings? Or endless blue as far as you can see?

LOOKING AT THE SKY, with no other goal than to observe it, is a **GREAT REMINDER** that no matter what else is happening, there is **BEAUTY AND WONDER AROUND US ALL THE TIME,** and it's **PRETTY AMAZING TO BE ALIVE.**

37 Find FUN in NOT-SO-FUN tasks.

It may be tough to muster up good feelings when you're taking out the trash or doing your homework or cleaning your room—but it's not impossible!

Instead of thinking about what else you wish you were doing, try being present as you complete the task. For example, as you walk the trash outside, feel the air on your skin and listen for any animals that might be nearby, like a bunny or a chipmunk. Imagine your muscles moving and your lungs filling with fresh air. Not up for whistling while you work? Then just try a little smile (or at the very least, not a frown).

Next try to frame the not-so-fun task in a way that acknowledges your good fortune. Think about how taking out the trash keeps your house a clean and comfortable place to live. Is the garbage in your neighborhood picked up by trash collectors? If so, think about how fortunate you are to have access to sanitation services like that when there are people in the world who don't.

Lastly, think of a way to make it fun! Can you skip the garbage all the way outside? Only hop on one foot? Try not to step on any cracks on the way out? Be silly! Make it a game!

INTRODUCE YOURSELF to NEW KIDS at SCHOOL.

38

It can be hard moving to a new place where you might not know your way around, have any friends, or even speak the language. You can make a huge difference to a new student at your school just by saying "Hi." Invite them to sit with you at lunch, be your partner in science class, or hang out after school. You might just make a new friend, and it feels great being able to help someone have a happier day!

39

TUNE IN
to Your
SENSES.

Take a walk today, or find a comfy spot to sit, and tune in to one of your five senses. What do you hear, taste, feel, smell, or see?

Make the Most of This Moment.

40

When things get hectic, it can be tough not to get lost in thought about what's to come, like next week's test, tomorrow's soccer practice, or even what's for dinner.

It can also be a challenge not to think about the past, like that time you tripped in the lunchroom, missed a shot in basketball, or what someone said to you earlier in the day.

You can think and think, but the future hasn't come yet, and the past has already happened, so there's nothing you can do to change it.

BUT, that doesn't mean you're powerless. Quite the opposite in fact. There's a lot you can do in this very moment.

Don't miss out on all the fun you can have *right now* by worrying too much about the past or fretting about the future. Get busy doing something that makes you happy—like reaching out to a friend, doing a craft, or reading a book—or something that helps prepare you for the future, like studying, practicing, or even just relaxing.

"Yesterday's the past, tomorrow's the future, but today is a gift. That's why it's called the present."
—Bil Keane, cartoonist

Practice
RANDOM ACTS
of Kindness.

41

Has anyone ever done something **out of the blue** that **brightened** your day? Maybe your **parents** put a note in your lunch bag, **someone you don't know** very well told you they like your new shoes, or a **friend** brought an extra snack to share with you at lunch.

Feels pretty great, right? You can pass that feeling on by practicing your own **random acts of kindness.**

"Throw kindness around like confetti." —Unknown

Enjoy!

10 Random Acts of Kindness

1 Sit with **someone** who is eating alone.

2 Hold the **door open** for someone.

3 Put a sticky note on the bathroom mirror in a public place with **a positive message** like "You look great!" or "I hope your day is as **amazing** as you are!"

4 Do your brother's or sister's **chores** for them.

5 If you see someone taking a picture of a group, **offer to take it** so that they can get in the photo.

7 Help a **neighbor** shovel snow or rake their leaves.

6 Need a certain **school supply** for one of your classes? **Bring an extra** in case someone **forgets** theirs.

8 Offer to **put someone else's cart back** at the grocery store.

10 If someone needs a day off from **walking their dog,** offer to do it for them.

9 Pay someone a **genuine compliment.**

and "Goodbye."

A great way to **SHOW APPRECIATION** for the people in your life is by enthusiastically **ACKNOWLEDGING THEIR PRESENCE.** That means that when they are arriving or leaving, **LOOK UP, MAKE EYE CONTACT, SAY "HI" OR "GOODBYE," AND EVEN CHAT FOR A FEW SECONDS.** Let it be known that you **see them** and it **matters to you** that they're there. They will feel more **valued,** and you'll both feel more **connected to one another.** Win-win!

43

DO A VICTORY DANCE!

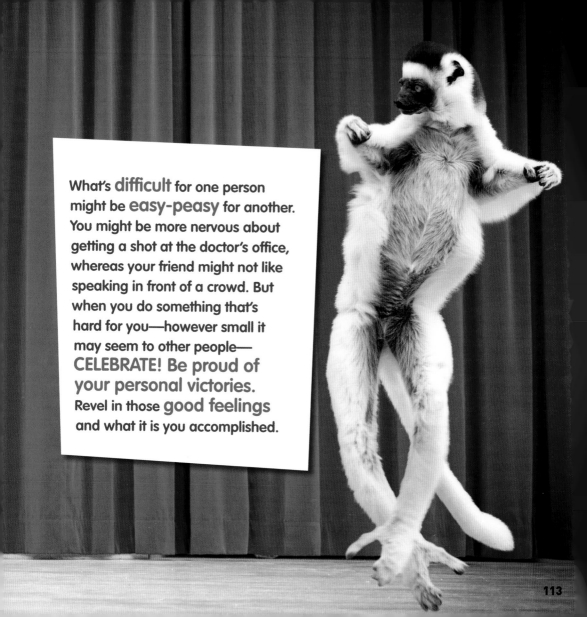

What's **difficult** for one person might be **easy-peasy** for another. You might be more nervous about getting a shot at the doctor's office, whereas your friend might not like speaking in front of a crowd. But when you do something that's hard for you—however small it may seem to other people—CELEBRATE! Be proud of your personal victories. Revel in those **good feelings** and what it is you accomplished.

MAKE *the* MOST *of Your* WEEKENDS.

44

Ahhh, weekends! **Two whole days** to do with what you please. It might be tempting to veg out in front of the TV for hours at a time, **but instead,** try to think of something you could do that would be more **meaningful** and **maximize the fun.**

 Here are five ideas to get the **brainstorm ball** rolling:

1. Look into visiting a local **museum.**
2. Organize a **big scavenger hunt** for a friend or family member. Leave clues around your house or neighborhood leading to a fun prize!
3. Pack a picnic and spend the afternoon at a park.
4. Sign up for a **run** or **walk** that **benefits a charity** you admire.
5. Take a **hike** with your **family** on a local nature trail.

Stop and smell

45

the roses, and the **cookies,** and the fresh-cut grass.

What's a **smell** that makes you **happy?** What's your **favorite food smell?** What do the **different seasons** smell like to you? What scent do you associate with your **favorite holiday?** Different scents can **energize** us, **calm** us, make us **hungry,** or **bring back memories.**

ASS Lemon VANILLA Bacon **the ocean** Honeysuckle Clean laundry
S Pizza RAIN Coconut **PEPPERMINT** Barbecue POPCORN coffee **ORANGE**
SS **Lemon** VANILLA Bacon the ocean Honeysuckle the
IN Coconut **PEPPERMINT** Barbecue POPCORN coffee NDER
ANILLA Bacon th PINE
ERMINT Barbecu FRESH-
an Honeysuckle za RAIN
RN coffee **ORAN** ANILLA
dry **A fire in the firepl** **ERMINT**
AVENDER Cookies Ba **ocean**
ace PINE TREES Ro POPCORN

GIVE IT A
>>GO! Now try making
a **list** of your **five**
favorite smells.

46

L♥VE

Love is the ultimate expression of gratitude. So, worry less about whether it's cool, and let yourself be enthusiastic about how much you love something or someone. And let yourself be loved in return!

Cherish the Changing of the SEASONS.

47

Depending on where you live in the world, you might get **snow that covers the ground** in a crunchy blanket during the winter months, or **leaves bursting with color** in the fall. But no matter where your hometown resides, each of the seasons—**summer, fall, winter, and spring**—brings lots to be thankful for.

WHAT CREATES SEASONS?

Earth rotates around the sun, and it takes one year for it to make one lap. As Earth rotates, it sometimes tilts toward the sun. Other times, it tilts away from the sun. Different parts of the planet experience the different seasons at different times—it all depends on where on Earth you live.

If it's summer where you live, then the part of Earth where you are is tilting toward the sun. The sun's rays are hitting that part of Earth more directly than they do at any other time of the year. So the days are warmer and longer. When it's winter where you are, the part of Earth where you live is tilted away from the sun. So the days are colder and shorter.

47 CHERISH THE CHANGING OF THE SEASONS.

Here are just a few of the many reasons to celebrate the seasons:

SPRING

1. **Shedding** a few layers (ahem, big winter coat!)
2. **Flowers**
3. **Longer days**
4. Plants turning **green** again and leaves returning
5. Lots of baby **animals** everywhere

SUMMER

1. **Watermelon**
2. Playing in the **sprinkler**
3. Eating **ice-cream cones** outside
4. **Summer break**
5. **Picnics**

1. Changing **leaves**
2. **Cooler** temperatures for playing outside
3. **Halloween**
4. New school **supplies**
5. Apple **pie**
   Apple **doughnuts**
   Apple **cider**

WINTER

1. **Snow** days
2. **Snuggling** up with a book
3. Fuzzy socks, **mittens,** and hats
4. Hot **chocolate**
5. Warm bubble **baths**

Make a *Gratitude Jar.*

48

Just by **PAYING ATTENTION** to what's **GOOD IN YOUR LIFE** and in your day—your blessings, your successes, your gifts and talents—you can **BECOME EVEN HAPPIER.** Pretty cool, right? Here's one way to do just that.

STEP 1:

Find an empty jar.

STEP 2:

Every time something happens that you're THANKFUL FOR (you got a good grade on a test, your dad made your favorite dinner, or your drama teacher said your monologue gave her goose bumps), WRITE IT DOWN on a little slip of paper, fold it, and PUT IT IN THE JAR.

STEP 3:

On days when you're feeling GRUMPY or SAD or like you need a pick-me-up, reach into the jar and read a few (or all!) of the papers you put in. Remember that on any day, in any situation, there is always something to be thankful for.

125

49 Get Out Into Nature

Nature is amazing. If you ever feel overwhelmed with what's going on in the news, your school, or even your house, go outside and sit still. Wait long enough, and you're sure to see something that reminds you that we are just one small part of life on Earth. While we stress about spelling tests and soccer tryouts and whether so-and-so likes so-and-so, squirrels are still scurrying busily, looking for nuts, fish are swimming in the streams, and little seedlings are sprouting into big, strong oak trees.

There are so many ways to express appreciation for the natural world— you can protect it, photograph it, paint it, write poems about it, teach others about it, and also, get out there and enjoy it!

(49) GET OUT INTO NATURE.

Here are a few ways to **experience** the magic that is **Mother Earth:**

1. Visit an orchard and pick fruit.

2. Put out a bird feeder and try to identify the birds that come to it.

3. Go for a nature walk.

4. Watch a sunrise or sunset.

5. Collect rocks or shells or acorns.

When Christian Thomas was five years old he became the youngest person to hike the entire length of the Appalachian Trail. He and his parents hiked the 2,189-mile (3,523-km) trail in eight months. Christian, who was given the trail nickname "Buddy Backpacker," then set his sights on the 2,660-mile (4,281-km) Pacific Crest Trail, which he completed in less than a year, and the 3,100-mile (4,989-km) Continental Divide Trail, which he just completed last year. At nine years old, he is the youngest person ever to complete all three of the United States' longest hiking trails, a feat called the Triple Crown. One way that Buddy likes to pass the time while hiking? By listening to music and podcasts on his headphones!

50 Take care of your things.

A great way to show that you care about your belongings is by doing your best to keep them in good condition. Accidents happen—it's easy to leave things on the bus, forget them out in the rain, or have them wind up in the hands of a younger sibling.

But, there are things you can do to keep your favorite stuff feeling fresh. For example:

- If you have a fishing pole that you love to use, make sure to rinse it with freshwater after each use, rinse your lures, and oil your gears if you're not going to use your pole for a while.

Just by doing a little research, you can become an almost-expert on how to keep the stuff you love in tip-top shape.

- If you notice a button's fallen off of your favorite coat, look up a how-to video online and sew it back on!

- If you have a bike you love, clean it so it doesn't get rusty, keep the tires inflated, and replace your brake pads when they get worn.

PRACTICE 51
Mindfulness.

MINDFULNESS is paying attention to the present moment, without judging it, on purpose.

To practice mindfulness, you bring your **awareness** to what's happening in this **very moment.** One way to do this is by tapping into one of your **five senses.** Another way to practice mindfulness is to pay attention to the **sensations in your body:** Is your stomach growling? How does the table feel beneath your palms? How warm and cozy do your feet feel in your socks?

Instead of thinking about what you did **five minutes ago,** or starting to plan what you'll be doing **five minutes from now,** being mindful means focusing on what's happening **RIGHT HERE, RIGHT NOW.**

Practicing mindfulness is a really important part of being thankful. When we practice mindfulness, we are **more likely** to notice and pay attention to **what's good** and **what's beautiful** in the **present moment.**

 **GIVE IT A GO!** Go for a *"thankful walk"* around your neighborhood or around a nearby park. While you walk, **pay careful attention** to what you feel, see, hear, and smell. Take notice of all the things you encounter that you're **thankful for.**

The way the air feels on your skin ... beautiful flowers ... the smell of grass ... chirping birds ... white fluffy clouds. If your **mind wanders,** gently bring it back to what you're experiencing on the walk and continue to take note of things that make **you feel grateful.**

133

Rejoice in SNOW DAYs!

52

Snowball fights, sledding, snow angels, hot chocolate, cozy movie marathons, mittens—and NO school!

Snow days = The. Best. Days. Ever!

(And if you live somewhere where you don't get snow, you can be thankful your swim practice won't be canceled, your shoes won't get soggy from slush, and you won't get stuck shoveling snow!)

The 2016 winner of the International Snow Sculpture Championships in Breckenridge, Colorado, U.S.A., was a piece called "Rhonda and Her Recycling Robo-Octopus." The sculpture, which was created by Team USA–Vermont, portrayed a fictional 14-year-old scientist named Rhonda, riding in her own invention, a Robo-Octopus that cleans the ocean floor. Fun fact: Each of the 16 teams starts with a 12-foot (3.7-m)-tall, 50,000-pound (22,680-kg) block of snow and has 65 hours to complete a sculpture.

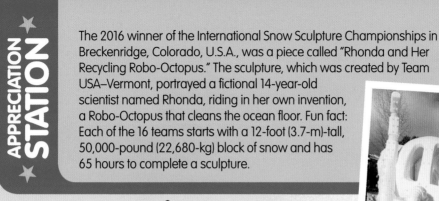

CATCH (and release) FIREFLIES.

These sparkly little insects can make a normal night feel magical. Fireflies, or lightning bugs, are one of the surefire signs summer has arrived. Their little glowing bodies light up backyards, baseball fields, forests, and big open meadows. Chase them, catch (and release) them, or just sit back and watch their twinkly light show.

WHY DO FIREFLIES GLOW?

Fireflies, a type of beetle, emerge at night and only live for about two months in the summertime. They prefer warm environments and moisture. You'll often see them in humid climates or near bodies of water. They have an organ near their stomach that takes in oxygen. The oxygen then mixes with a substance called luciferin, which is already present in their systems, to create light.

PLAY.

Sure, you may not be into the same toys you played with when you were little. Maybe you don't even play with toys at all. **BUT YOU ARE NEVER TOO OLD TO PLAY.**

So what is play, exactly?
Play is something you do for
no other reason than to have fun.

And while your goal might be just to have a great time
(AND YOU WILL!), research has shown that some of
the BEST learning can come from playing. Play teaches
you HOW TO THINK OUTSIDE THE BOX, be more CREATIVE, keep
going when things get tough, WORK AS A TEAM, bond with others, be
present, and HAVE FUN!

Here Are **10** Ways to Infuse Your Day With a Little More PLaY.

1. Dust off your old coloring books, sharpen some crayons or colored pencils, and spend time trying to stay inside the lines.

2. Get some friends and neighbors together for a big group game like charades, flashlight tag, or Frisbee.

3. Bust out some Play-Doh or clay. Try making animals, shapes, or figures. Bonus points for sculpting a self-portrait.

4. Institute family game nights.

5. Check out a play script from the library, get a group of friends together, and act it out.

6 Construct a model airplane, boat, or house.

7 Put together a jigsaw puzzle with your friends or family.

8 Decorate cookies or a cake, just because. No special occasion necessary.

9 Go bowling, play laser tag, or check out an arcade.

10 Make a goofy video with your friends—act out skits, pretend to be talk show hosts, or make a cooking tutorial.

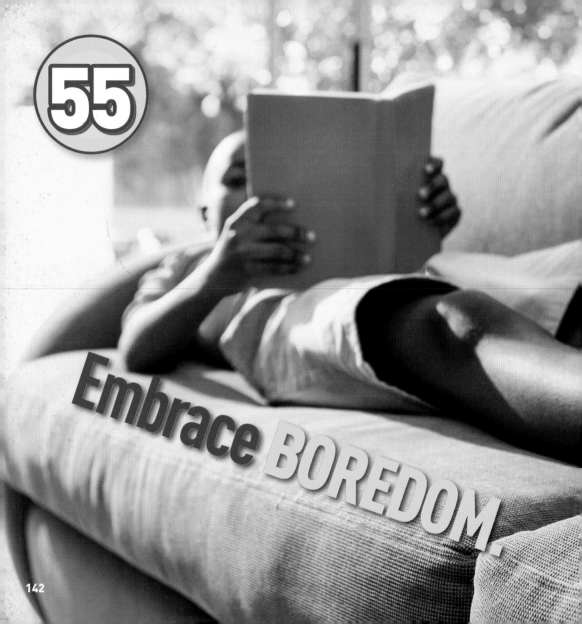

55

Embrace BOREDOM.

DO YOU REMEMBER TWO WEEKS AGO WHEN YOU WERE SUPER STRESSED? You had chores you had to do, two tests to study for, and a big project due the next day. Well, now you are actually bored. With, like, nothing to do.

BUT INSTEAD OF WHINING AND COMPLAINING, JUST BE BORED. BLISSFULLY.

Downtime—for both your body and your mind—is important and healthy. Next time you feel boredom settling in, be thankful that you have a moment when there's nowhere you need to be and nothing you need to be doing. Let your mind wander, read a book, come up with creative ways to entertain yourself, or just lie in the grass and watch the clouds pass overhead.

56

LOOK IN THE MIRROR AND FIND SOMETHING YOU LIKE.

The way your hair looks today. The gap between your front teeth. Your freckles. Your eyes (which look just like your mom's). Your smile. Your long legs. Your short legs. Your ears (that you just learned how to wiggle).

It can be anything. But, every day, find something.

Sit Down for Breakfast.

57

Instead of rushing out the door with a bagel or a cereal bar, wake up a few minutes earlier so that you can actually enjoy your breakfast. Try this for one week and see how it feels: Sit down with your breakfast, think about what you'd like to accomplish today, and enjoy the food that's providing your body with the nourishment and energy you need to reach your goals.

Check out these dishes you might see on breakfast menus around the world.

Where: Honduras

Breakfast Fave:
Fried eggs, refried beans, tangy sour cream, cheese, avocado, sweet fried plantains, and tortillas

Where: Japan

Breakfast Fave: Miso soup and pickled vegetables

Where: Morocco

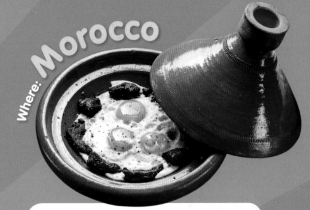

Breakfast Fave: A dish called *khlea* made from small strips of dried beef mixed with fried eggs

Where: England

Breakfast Fave: Eggs, grilled tomatoes, sausage, and baked beans

Where: China

Breakfast Fave: Rice porridge

147

58

TREASURE the STORIES Your FAMILY TELLS AGAIN and AGAIN.

149

Be Part of the Solution.

There will be many times in your life when you notice things that aren't right or that could be better. In these moments, look for opportunities to help. Look for ways to be part of the solution.

That's exactly what **Gitanjali Rao,** winner of the **2017 Discovery Education 3M Young Scientist Challenge,** did! When she was just 11 years old, she learned about the water crisis happening in **Flint, Michigan, U.S.A.** The water crisis began in 2014, when it was discovered that there were high levels of lead in the drinking water, which can make people very, very sick. The people of Flint still can't drink the water that comes from their faucets and have been told they may not be able to until 2020. "I did some research, and I realized it wasn't only in Flint—there are more than 5,000 water systems in the U.S. with lead contamination," says Gitanjali. "That's when it kind of sank in that it's a pretty big problem."

So, Gitanjali put her love of science to work and invented a device, called **Tethys,** that can quickly detect lead in water.

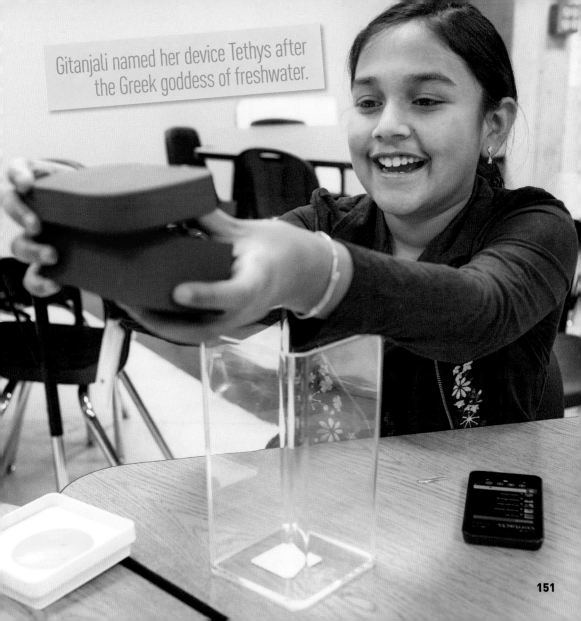

Gitanjali named her device Tethys after the Greek goddess of freshwater.

Q: What inspired you to create Tethys?

A: I had originally been introduced to the Flint water crisis through my STEM (science, technology, engineering, and mathematics) lab. But I didn't think about creating a device until I saw my parents testing for lead in our water, which made a real-world connection for me. I thought [that] if it's taking this long to test for lead in our house, then imagine how long it would take to test in schools or places like Flint, Michigan, and every household. So that's when I developed my idea for my device.

Q: How did you come up with the ideas for the technical parts?

A: I follow the MIT Department of Materials Science and Engineering research page to see the latest developments in technology. That's where I found out that there is a way to use carbon nanotube sensors in order to detect hazardous gases. And I realized that if we can use carbon nanotubes to detect hazardous gases, why not extend it to a liquid medium and use them to detect lead in water? So, I did two months of planning, and then I was picked as one of the top 10 finalists for the Discovery Education 3M Young Scientist Challenge. When I met my 3M mentor, she helped me take the idea and turn it into real life.

Q: What advice would you give to other young people who want to be a part of the solution, too?

A: In the beginning of the process, I didn't know if I really wanted to try because it required complex equipment, and I didn't know for sure that I could actually accomplish it other than proposing my idea. My instant reaction was that if I didn't accomplish it, I would feel really bad about myself, so I thought about skipping it and trying something simpler. But then I decided to go for it! If I didn't understand something, it was OK. I had a mentor who guided me, or I asked for help. The worst response I could have gotten was a "no", but if I didn't try, I never would have known if it worked. I'd like to tell other people who have an idea but who are hesitant to execute it to not be afraid to try. Failure is just another step to success. There are people who are ready to help. All we need to do is ask!

Q: **What are you working on now? What's next for you?**

A: I'm working on scale testing on Tethys, in partnership with Denver Water. I recently changed my sensor design for better usability. I have also enhanced it to allow data upload and analysis to potentially create a heat map that shows locations with more or less lead levels. This may help people take action. In parallel, I am researching advances in genetic engineering and potential solutions to the problem of adolescent depression. I call this my "Happiness Detector."

What do you like to do when you're NOT studying and practicing science?

- I play two sports—I fence and I swim.

- I like to go for walks around my neighborhood; we've got a nice trail in my backyard.

- I go for bike rides with my friends.

- My family's a big baking family. We don't bake cakes or pies—instead, we make desserts from all around the world, like macaroons, baklava, and marzipan.

60 Be a bookworm.

Congrats! You picked up the book in your hands, so you're off to a good start!

There is so much to be thankful for when it comes to books, including ...

- Snuggling up on a rainy day with **nothing else to do but read.**
- The **anticipation** of waiting for a **new book** to come out in your **favorite series.**
- Knowing that no matter where you are in the world, you can learn more about **new people** and **places** and **ideas,** just by reading a book!
- Learning all sorts of awesome **new vocabulary words.**
- Knowing that even when you're going through something tough, you can probably find a book about someone who has **experienced something similar.**
- Cool **bookmarks!**
- The **suspense!** The **tears!** The *awws!* The **laughs!**

Jake Marcionette is the youngest author to ever have a book on the *New York Times* Best Seller list. Jake wrote and published his first book when he was only 12 years old! The book, *Just Jake,* is a funny adventure about a sixth grader whose life gets upended when he moves to a new state and school. Jake started his writing career during summer breaks from school, when his mom had him and his sister write every day, from breakfast until lunch. What started as sort of a pain eventually turned into a passion, and now Jake has written three books in the Just Jake series and even has plans for a new line of books.

155

Learn More About Your
Family's
History.

61

Give thanks for your ancestors by learning more about where you came from.

Ask your parents and grandparents to help you fill out a family tree. When you add a new name, ask around to see if people in your family know any stories or information about that person.

Also, ask your parents and grandparents about what life was like when they were little.

You can ask BIG questions:

What were some of the greatest advancements and inventions that happened when you were growing up?

What were your hopes and dreams as kids?

Ask simpler questions to get a sense of what their lives were like and how things have changed:

What was your favorite treat to buy at the store?

What was your favorite toy or game to play when you were my age?

62

LOOK FOR A LESSON IN STRUGGLES.

You might be saying, **"C'MON, NOT EVERYTHING HAS A SILVER LINING."** And you're right, **NOT EVERYTHING DOES.** Some things just plain stink. But most difficult situations come **JAM-PACKED WITH LESSONS.** In fact, **WE LEARN THE MOST ABOUT OURSELVES,** and others, as we **NAVIGATE TOUGH TIMES.** Challenges, failures, mistakes, disagreements, heartbreak, jealousy, fear—they all offer **OPPORTUNITIES** to become a **BETTER PERSON, OPEN YOUR HEART, BE MORE COMPASSIONATE, COMMUNICATE BETTER,** and more.

The **next time** you encounter a difficult person or a challenging situation, **ask yourself:**

- What can I learn from this?
- What can I do to be better suited for a similar situation in the future?
- What can I take from this that might help me become a better me?

Celebrate today.

63

YOU CAN'T DO **anything** ABOUT WHAT HAPPENED **yesterday.** YOU **can't** DO ANYTHING ABOUT WHAT'S **going to happen** TOMORROW. BUT THERE IS **one day** THAT'S WITHIN YOUR **control—today.** SO GO AHEAD AND **create a great one.**

64

And Celebrate That Tomorrow Is a *New Day.*

MAYBE TODAY WAS HARD. MAYBE IT WAS *really* hard. BUT, GUESS WHAT? TOMORROW YOU GET TO start all over again. CLEAN SLATE. FRESH START. New day.

65

Bask in Bubble Baths.

Baths are a great way to have some alone time to soak in the day's events, ease muscle tension, and reflect and enjoy the moment. Studies have even found that baths can help improve your mood.

Add bubbles to the equation, and you get all of the great benefits of a bath plus bubble beards and bubble wigs. Score!

Be a WILD ANIMAL Advocate.

LIONS AND TIGERS AND BEARS—OH, MY! IT'S PRETTY AWESOME THAT WE GET TO ROAM THE SAME EARTH AS THESE MAJESTIC CREATURES.

All wild animals deserve to live healthy, happy, wild lives. Unfortunately, there are many species around the globe in danger of going extinct. So, to honor them and to show our gratitude for their existence, it's up to us to do the best we can to make sure our actions don't have a harmful impact on them.

Even though you might not come in contact with many giraffes, gorillas, whales, rhinos, or elephants, there are things you can do in your everyday life to protect wild animals.

Here are just a few ways you can help:

Do your research.
Do a quick search on an animal you're interested in. Find out more about its habitat, the food it eats, and any threats to its well-being.

Support organizations that protect wildlife.
Hold a car wash, bake sale, or neighborhood-wide garage sale to raise money and awareness.

Recycle.
Recycling can reduce the need to cut down more trees, which protects forests and the animals that live in them.

Don't litter.
Never throw trash on the ground and also pick up any that you see. Wild animals, like birds and turtles, can mistake trash for food, which can cause them to get sick or even choke. Plastic trash or wire can get wrapped around an animal's beak, leg, or body, and, if eaten, can clog the digestive tract. Even spit-out gum can get stuck in an animal's fur or on its wings.

Don't buy products that harm animals.
These include clothes or jewelry that use endangered animal furs, ivory, rhinoceros horn, tortoise shell, or crocodile skins.

Encourage your family not to use harmful chemicals on your lawn.
Pesticides and herbicides can hurt pets and honeybees, and when it rains, these chemicals get washed into bodies of water, which isn't healthy for the animals living there.

Buy cruelty-free toiletries.
These are products that were not tested on animals.

Write to your members of Congress.
Let them know that it's important to you that they support laws and legislation that protect wild animals.

Biodiversity is the variety of life on Earth, or within a particular ecosystem. Each living thing affects the health and existence of other living things. For example, who knew that we have bats to thank every time we eat corn on the cob? It's true! Bats eat pests, like earworm larvae, that harm corn crops. That's just one example, but all life is connected, which is why each and every species is important and in need of our protection.

67 Always say

Here are a few folks who probably deserve a "Thanks!" today:

Whoever refills your water or brings you food at a restaurant

Coaches, teachers, or instructors who inspire or motivate you

The people who serve food in your cafeteria

Write a Fan Letter.

68

Think of someone in the public eye who INSPIRES you, ENTERTAINS you, or just plain MAKES YOU HAPPY. Then, LET THEM KNOW! It could be an ATHLETE, a POLITICIAN, an ACTOR, a SINGER, a COMEDIAN, an AUTHOR, an ACTIVIST, or anyone else.

Ask an adult to help you find an address where you can send them a token of your APPRECIATION. You could WRITE A NOTE or a POEM, PAINT A PICTURE, or MAKE A VIDEO of you singing a song.

However you choose to communicate it, the most IMPORTANT thing is that you let them know WHAT THEY MEAN TO YOU and that you're THANKFUL for them!

69

Savor a Scoop
(or two or three) of
Ice Cream.

Whether creamy or crunchy, wild and wacky, or sweet and simple, ice cream is always awesome. And whatever form it takes—an ice-cream sundae, ice-cream float, ice-cream cake, or a sweet, drippy cone—it is bound to be delicious. Next time you eat ice cream, slow down and celebrate each bite.

174

APPRECIATION ★ STATION

The two founders of Ben & Jerry's Ice Cream, Ben Cohen and Jerry Greenfield, met when they were in the seventh grade. Years later, as adults, they decided to try starting a business together. They landed on the idea of an ice-cream shop after they discovered that the equipment needed for their first business idea—a bagel shop—was too expensive. Ben and Jerry, who are still best friends to this day, were the inventors of chocolate chip cookie dough ice cream, which is still their most popular flavor worldwide. But, beyond the deliciousness they'd put out into the world, Ben and Jerry were determined to do good. In 1985, they started the Ben & Jerry's Foundation, committing 7.5 percent of the company's profits to philanthropy efforts that support social justice, protect the environment, and support sustainable food systems.

10 WILD AND WACKY ICE-CREAM FLAVORS

1. Sweet corn
2. Huckleberry
3. Goat cheese
4. Cereal milk
5. Garlic
6. Mustard
7. Avocado
8. Cinnamon toast
9. Lobster
10. Bacon

175

70

Learn **MORE** About Other **PEOPLE**... and **CELEBRATE** What Makes Us **DIFFERENT** and the **SAME.**

One powerful way to practice gratitude for humans around the world, including the ways that we are different and the ways that we are similar, is to learn about other people, the richness of different cultures, and the wild range of human experiences.

Meet **National Geographic Young Explorer Asha Stuart.** She has made it her life's work to do just that. As a **documentary filmmaker** she observes what life is like for people around the world and then she creates a record of it that can be shared with others.

Q What is a project that you've worked on that you've felt particularly proud of?

A I recently finished a documentary called *The Lost Tribe of Africa*. It's about the Siddi tribe in India, which many people don't know exists. Sometime between the 15th and 19th centuries, they were forcibly taken from their homes in Africa and brought to India where they were made slaves. Today the Siddi people continue to struggle to find their own identity in a country that never wanted them there.

Q Do you remember one of the first documentary films you saw that had an impact on you?

A *Nanook of the North* is the first documentary I remember seeing. It's about the ways of life of some ancient Inuit tribes. It was the first time that I had ever seen indigenous people on film. For some reason, that this ancient tribal culture could come alive for the modern viewer was pure magic to me. The documentary allowed me to get a glimpse of their real, raw lives and of that time in history.

Inuit are indigenous people of northern Canada and parts of Greenland and Alaska.

Q What is it that you love about learning about other people, places, cultures, and customs?

A Learning about other places that are completely different from my own reminds me that there is something fundamental about the human experience that binds us all together. Everyone wants things like basic respect, a decent life, and good relationships, and although it may look different in my country than it does in yours, at the core we want the same things.

Q What about your work most excites you?

A It might sound cliché, but it's true: Meeting new people all around the world is what most excites me about my work. I feel like as a documentarian I've been granted access to many places that others would never have access to, and for me that feels like such a privilege.

Q What qualities does one need to be a great documentary filmmaker?

A Listening, listening, listening. We conduct such in-depth interviews about people's communities and their lives, and typically when we go on assignment, we're dealing with something we don't know much about before we get there. So listening becomes essential to the task itself, as well as being a critical aspect of mutual respect and becoming part of the communities we work with.

Q When do you feel most grateful when you're creating your work?

A When the work brings visibility about a subject, people, or a place that would otherwise go relatively unnoticed. I feel especially thankful when that visibility gains traction into something actionable that brings about much needed change in a community.

Q How do you think learning about other people and the way they experience life relates to practicing gratitude?

A I feel very grateful that people trust me enough to open up and share their intimate lives and thoughts and feelings. I think that the differences between cultures and people is what makes the world such a rich and exciting place. And for that I think many of us are extremely grateful.

71

Get to know your unique point of view.

Your Life EXPERIENCES +
Your THOUGHTS + Your FEELINGS
= Your POINT OF VIEW

Knowing what you **think** and **feel**, and **why**, is a great way to **APPRECIATE** what makes **you** uniquely **YOU.**

72

And get to know the unique point of view of others.

ALL AROUND THE WORLD, HUMANS HAVE SUCH **DIFFERENT DAY-TO-DAY EXPERIENCES. WE SPEAK** DIFFERENT LANGUAGES, **EAT** DIFFERENT FOODS, **PLAY** DIFFERENT GAMES, AND **CELEBRATE DIFFERENT HOLIDAYS.**

But, when you sit down with someone and **talk to them,** you will find that there's **much about us that's the same.** Most folks love their families and want to be healthy and happy and safe, have fun, and have access to opportunities to help them **live their best lives.**

Learning about how **other people think** and **feel** is a **GREAT WAY** to show thanks for how **diverse** people are.

73

GET LOST IN SPACE.

Sometimes, it's **IMPORTANT** to get a little **perspective** about our place in the **UNIVERSE**. So let's start here:

EARTH, the planet where we LIVE, is one of eight planets that rotate around our sun, MAKING OUR SOLAR SYSTEM. This solar system is just ONE SMALL part of a much LARGER galaxy called the MILKY WAY. In the whole universe—which includes all existing matter and space—there are more stars than grains of sand on all the beaches on Earth. That's at least a BILLION TRILLION STARS!

We are just little specks in what is an almost UNIMAGINABLY GINORMOUS universe.

Milky Way galaxy

YOU ARE HERE

Next time you go outside at night, take a few minutes to look up at the sky. THINK about how, in the big scheme of things, each one of us is so very small and *SO VERY PRECIOUS.*

That we exist—right here, right now— is AMAZING.

74 VOLUNTEER.

10 Awesome Ways to VOLUNTEER

1. **Walk dogs** at a local animal shelter.
2. **Help sort** and **box food** at a food pantry.
3. **Visit** or **play games** with older folks at a **retirement home.**
4. **Serve meals** at a homeless shelter.
5. Hold a **bake sale** for your favorite **charity.**
6. Help out with **after-school events** at the **library** in your town.
7. Participate in a **trash cleanup** with an environmental organization.
8. **Donate** your old clothes, toys, and sports equipment to a **local shelter** or **Goodwill.**
9. **Tutor** younger kids in reading.
10. Participate in a **run** or **walk** to raise money and awareness for a cause you care about.

A huge way to give thanks for your own blessings, gifts, and good fortune is to help other people. Be on the lookout for opportunities in your neighborhood, community, or school to lend a helping hand. Then, consider volunteering your time and energy with a local organization that could use your help.

75

Train yourself to see

beauty everywhere.

It's there if you look for it.

76

Be Amazed by Your Brain by Your Ability (and Your Ability to Change It!).

The HUMAN BRAIN is INCREDIBLE. This THREE-POUND (1.4-kg) POWERHOUSE contains BILLIONS of nerve cells that receive information, process it, then relay messages throughout the body in SPLIT SECONDS. Your brain is the CONTROL CENTER FOR EVERYTHING happening in your body—the way your MUSCLES MOVE, your FEELINGS and MOODS, even HOW FAST YOUR HEART BEATS.

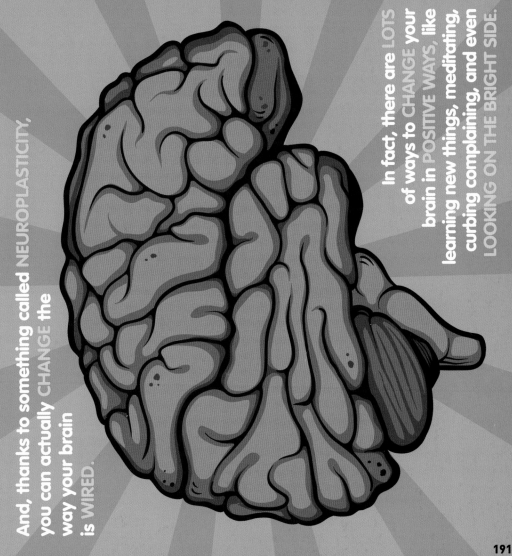

And, thanks to something called NEUROPLASTICITY, you can actually CHANGE the way your brain is WIRED.

In fact, there are LOTS of ways to CHANGE your brain in POSITIVE WAYS, like learning new things, meditating, curbing complaining, and even LOOKING ON THE BRIGHT SIDE.

191

Find **Awesome**

When you're looking to be inspired, motivated, or challenged to be better, find someone to look up to. This could be a teacher, a sibling, a politician, a parent, an athlete, or an actor. They might be someone you know or someone you've only ever seen on TV or read about in history books.

Once you've found someone you think is pretty great, do some research. Read interviews the person has given, check out a biography from the library, or ask the person to meet so you can pick their brain.

The idea isn't to try to be just like them, but instead to find little nuggets of wisdom, pieces of advice, or tips of the trade that can educate and inspire you on your own personal journey to greatness, and to ultimately being the best YOU.

ROLE Models.

Four **Awesome** Folks to **Look Up To:**

Who they are:
Malala Yousafzai

What they do:
Activist/Author/Oxford University student

A couple reasons they're awesome:
When she was 15 years old, Malala was shot by the Taliban in Pakistan for advocating for girls' education. She is the youngest winner of the Nobel Peace Prize, and with her father, she founded the Malala Fund, which aims to give all girls access to education.

Who they are: Lin-Manuel Miranda

What they do: Composer/Lyricist/Actor

A couple reasons they're awesome: By creating the hit musical *Hamilton*, he taught loads of fans about Alexander Hamilton, one of America's Founding Fathers. He's also raised millions of dollars for the Hispanic Federation, which supports Hispanic families and Latino institutions and has provided tremendous support to Puerto Rico after Hurricane Maria.

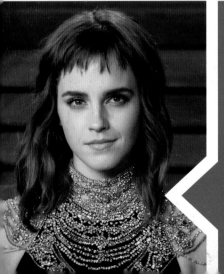

Who they are: Emma Watson

What they do: Actress/UN Women Goodwill Ambassador

A couple reasons they're awesome: Not only did she star as Hermione in the awesome Harry Potter movies, she is an advocate for girls' education and women's rights around the world. As a UN Women Goodwill Ambassador, she's spoken on behalf of the organization HeForShe, which asks men to speak out about gender equality, and she also started a feminist book club on Goodreads called Our Shared Shelf that anyone can join.

Who they are: LeBron James

What they do: Professional basketball player/Community leader/Education advocate/Philanthropist

A couple reasons they're awesome:
Not only is he one of the greatest basketball players of all time, LeBron cares deeply about helping others and giving back to the community. Recently, with his nonprofit, the LeBron James Family Foundation, he created the I Promise School, in Akron, Ohio, U.S.A., where he grew up. The aim of this innovative school is to help students who are at risk of falling behind their peers and who would benefit from some extra help. In addition to a top-notch education, students at the I Promise School will receive additional types of assistance to help them succeed, like free meals and snacks, a bicycle and helmet, and college tuition.

78
Admire Art.

Great art has the power to stir up big, even unexpected feelings. Great art is **a window** into **another world;** it can give you a glimpse into how someone else experiences life. A piece of art can make you **mad,** it can make you **sad,** it can **inspire you,** or help you **feel less alone.**

TO ADMIRE ART IS TO APPRECIATE IT.

Going to a **museum** and **doing a full tour** is **GREAT,** but consider, as an alternative, doing a **deep dive** into **ONE ARTIST** or even **ONE WORK OF ART.** Read about the **artist's life** and **work,** the **techniques** and **tools** he or she used, how their **style evolved over time,** what **inspired** them, and what was going on in the world when your **FAVORITE** work was created.

197

BE A GOOD

A great way to show thanks to someone in your life is by being a good listener when they speak. Put away any distractions (like electronics or toys), don't interrupt, and ask thoughtful follow-up questions to make sure you understand what they're saying.

80 Try Your BEST NOT TO WASTE.

You know the feeling: When you're eating a crazy-good cookie, you don't want to drop a single crumb. If you only have one hour to play at the park, you don't want to spend a single minute dillydallying. And, if you've worked hard to save money, you don't want to blow it on something silly that you don't really want.

Wasting something, or using it up carelessly, is the opposite of really appreciating it. So, here are a few easy ways to conserve precious resources:

→ Turn off lights and electronics when you leave a room.

→ Take shorter showers and turn off the faucet while you brush your teeth.

→ Walk or ride your bike instead of taking a car.

→ Cook only as much food as you're going to eat or save leftovers to eat later.

→ Learn how to fix things instead of throwing them away.

→ Use reusable grocery and lunch bags.

→ Put down your electronics.

Americans produce an estimated 4.5 pounds (2 kg) of garbage A DAY, and much of that is food packaging. Think about it: water bottles, wrappers, straws, cardboard boxes, plastic containers—not to mention plastic grocery bags, which take years to decompose in landfills. So, waste-free stores are now opening around the world that do away with packaging altogether. Customers bring their own reusable containers, like canning jars, cloth bags, or canisters, and then fill them with loose foods—everything from beans and cereal to spices and candy. Ta-ta for now, trash!

81

Celebrate Sunshine.

82

And REVEL in the RAIN.

Make Someone a HOMEMADE Gift.

If you want to **thank someone** for something they did, or just show them that **you're thankful for them in your life**, give them a **superspecial** token of your appreciation, by **making it yourself.**

FIVE HANDMADE **Thank-You** GIFT IDEAS:

1. A personalized greeting card
2. **A knit plush or pillow**
3. Homemade cookies
4. **A clay bowl, figurine, or jewelry**
5. A homemade picture frame (see the next page for instructions)

GIVE IT A GO! Here's how to make a **homemade picture frame.**

YOU WILL NEED:

- Four large craft sticks
- Glue
- Beads, buttons, pom-poms, shells, or any other decorations you like
- Paint (and paint pens and glitter if you'd like)
- Ruler
- A photo to frame

DIRECTIONS:

STEP 1: Paint the craft sticks however you'd like and let them dry.

Step 2: Glue the craft sticks in a square. Let the glue dry completely.

Step 3: Then, decorate your frame. Use shells, pom-poms, buttons, glitter, stickers—anything you like!

Step 4: Using a ruler, measure the frame opening.

Step 5: Carefully cut the photo to fit the opening in your frame.

Step 6: Glue the photo to the back of the frame so that the picture shows from the front.

Voilà! You've made a superspecial and heartfelt homemade gift.

"Never be afraid to raise your voice for honesty and truth and compassion against injustice and lying and greed. If people all over the world ... would do this, it would change the earth." —William Faulkner

SPEAK UP
FOR THOSE IN NEED.

Show gratitude for your voice and your ability to speak out by talking about issues and people that need help and attention. You have the power to create positive change, and it all starts with the simple act of talking about the things that need to be better.

- When you see someone being bullied → Tell a teacher or a trusted adult.
- When you see an injustice happening in your community → Talk about it with friends and family, reach out to your mayor or governor, call your representatives in Congress to voice your concern, or write a letter to your local newspaper.
- When you see animals in need → Bring attention to the cause by telling others, posting photos, or holding a fund-raiser.
- When you learn about something happening in the country or in the world that needs attention → Ask questions about it in class, post about it on your social media, bring it up at the dinner table, and brainstorm ways you can make a difference.

85

When You Have More Than You Need—

SHARE.

Whatever it may be—
food, pencils, quarters for the vending machine—give a little when you can.

86 Celebrate

Being thankful extends beyond just what is happening in your own life. Think about someone you care about who is doing well and be thankful that good things are happening for them. Then, let them know you're excited for them. Consider writing them a note of congratulations, picking them a flower, or bringing them a cookie. They'll feel great, and so will you!

other people's
achievements.

Seek out—then share—stuff that makes you smile.

87

Be on the lookout for good news, funny jokes, inspiring stories, or aww-inducing cuteness. Then, pass on that positivity by sharing it with friends and family. A photo of a porcupine and a bulldog who became BFFs? Sure! An inspiring story about a local hero? Yes, please! A five-year-old geography expert? You betcha! Making someone else smile is sometimes just a newspaper clipping or a mouse click away!

Give Thanks to Unsung Heroes! Like Bees!

88

When you don't see all of the hard work being done to make something, it can be easy to take it for granted. This is true for lots of things—like birthday parties, school projects, or choir recitals. Sure, you may really enjoy the final product, but you might not fully appreciate the sweat, tears, and hours of work that went into creating it.

Take for example—**bees.** While we are going about our days, bees are busy work, work, working away. Some people even think of bees as a bother and wish they'd just buzz off.

But bees are actually **tiny, winged superheroes.**

Not only do bees produce **delicious honey,** more than **one-third** of the **world's crops** and more than **90 percent of wild plants** are dependent on bee pollination. Bees pollinate by transferring pollen and seeds from one flower to another, which **fertilizes** the plant so that it can grow the things that we later eat—like apples, oranges, mangoes, broccoli, cucumbers, and pumpkins (to name a few).

In recent years, lots of bees have disappeared, which worries scientists and farmers. They think there are a number of factors contributing to the decrease, including climate change, pesticide use, and habitat loss.

More Bees, Please! Five Fun Facts About Bees!

1. There are more than 20,000 species of bees in the world.

2. Bees aren't the only pollinating species—in fact, there are more than 200,000 different species around the world that act as pollinators, including moths, butterflies, birds, bats, and even some small mammals (like some monkeys!).

3. In places around the world where **bee populations** have dwindled, like some parts of China, **farmers pollinate** their flowers and crops **by hand.**

4. The average **worker bee** lives for just **five to six weeks.** During this time, she'll produce around a **twelfth of a teaspoon** of honey.

5. Honeybees have **six legs, four wings,** and **five eyes** (**two** large compound eyes on either side of their head as well as **three** simple light-detecting eyes in the center).

GIVE IT A
>> GO!

If you want to **help out** the **bee population,** plant **flowers** or **plants** in your yard that are **native to your area** and are a **variety of shapes and colors.** Make sure there are plants blooming **during each season,** so there's always **nectar** and **pollen** for the bees to eat, and only use **natural pesticides.**

89 Have Empathy.

You practice empathy **when you put yourself in someone else's shoes,** when you think about how it would feel to be them and **experience what they're experiencing.**

You can **practice empathy during happy times**—how would it feel to win the class presidential election?—**and hard times**—how would it feel to be left out of a game at recess?

If someone in your life is going through a hard time, **think about what it might feel like** to be them right now. If you were going through something similar, **what might brighten your spirits or make you feel less alone?**

Even **animals** appear to be capable of **feeling** and **expressing empathy for one another.** In fact, a recent study done at Emory University in the United States found that when one prairie vole was **exposed to stress,** another prairie vole would often **comfort** and **console** them by grooming them. Aww!

223

Share your skills.

90

EVERYONE'S good at *something.*

What's your *special skill?*
KNITTING?
SINGING?
TELLING JOKES?

Think of ways to USE YOUR SKILLS and TALENTS to *help other people,* or at the very least *bring a smile to their face.*

91

Celebrate EVERYTHING.

Celebrate holidays, celebrate birthdays, celebrate days of the week that end in "y." Celebrate little things, celebrate big things, and celebrate everything in between.

"The more you celebrate your life, the more there is in life to celebrate." —Oprah Winfrey

Don't SWEAT the SMALL STUFF.

92

Hey, stuff happens. It's **absolutely OK** to feel sad or mad or frustrated when it seems things **aren't going your way.**

But, **even when times are tough,** it's still possible to **feel thankful.**

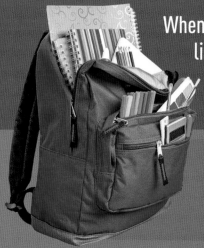

When something happens that gets you feeling like, *Woe is me!*, **think about how things could be worse,** then **be grateful they're not.** For example:

- You forgot your homework at home. → **It could be worse!** → Your teacher **could have said** you'd receive a 0, **but** instead you get to bring it in tomorrow for partial credit.

- You got mud all over your new shoes. → **It could be worse!** → You **could have** slipped in the mud and been covered head to toe (**plus,** you can probably wash the shoes).

- You broke your brother's fidget spinner. → **It could be worse!** → You **could have** broken his computer or his game console, which would have been **a lot** more expensive to fix.

Take a minute to be **thankful** that things **aren't worse.** Things are **looking up** already!

93

Write a GOOD REVIEW.

If you've had a great experience somewhere, like at a restaurant, store, or a cool museum, tell the owners, managers, or staff about your positive experience. Write a nice note on a comment card, send them an e-mail, or even ask your parents to help you write an online review.

95

ORGANIZE A TRASH

CLEANUP.

SHOW YOUR **APPRECIATION** FOR THE PLACES YOU **ENJOY** BY GATHERING A GROUP AND **PICKING UP TRASH** THERE. (DON'T FORGET TO **WEAR GLOVES!**)

96

Appreciate Life's Many Surprises.

LIFE has a way of *KEEPING YOU ON YOUR TOES.* You *NEVER KNOW* what's around the **next corner.** It might be a **wild adventure,** a *FUN* new *FRIENDSHIP,* or a **life-changing** *OPPORTUNITY. EVERY* new day has the **potential** for all sorts of **surprising** *TWISTS* and *TURNS.*

97

Be DAZZLED by BEAUTIFUL

Whether they're the as-big-as-your-head roses growing in your neighbor's garden, a rainbow patch of wildflowers brightening the side of the highway, or one lone dandelion growing up from a crack in the sidewalk, take a moment to stop and appreciate little bits of beautiful wherever they may be.

And, while you're at it, check out these three kooky blooms.

The purple passionflower, or maypop *(Passiflora incarnata)*, grows on a vine, is often found growing wild in the southeastern United States, and is a big favorite of butterflies.

The monkey face orchid *(Dracula simia)* is found in the forests of Ecuador and smells like oranges.

The happy alien flower *(Calceolaria uniflora)*, also known as Darwin's slipper, is found in South America and was discovered by Charles Darwin.

98

BE IN AWE.

The world is breathtaking. Life is incredible. Your capacity to do amazing things is big and real and awesome. Don't forget to sit still every once in a while and wonder at it all.

99 PAY IT

One COOL WAY to show your GRATITUDE for a good deed someone does for you is by PAYING IT FORWARD, or performing the same, or a similar, good deed for SOMEONE ELSE.

FORWARD.

For example, if someone loans you a pencil in class, to PAY IT FORWARD, you would bring an extra pencil the next day to loan to someone who doesn't have one. Or, if someone teaches you how to beat a level on your video game or how to jump double Dutch, to PAY IT FORWARD, you would teach someone else.

PAYING IT FORWARD *is a great way to keep the* GOOD GRATITUDE VIBES *flowing.*

Take This Thankful QUIZ.

If ever you're having trouble coming up with reasons to be thankful, hopefully this quiz will prompt some new ideas. Just grab a piece of paper and jot down your answers.

1.
Something **silly** I'm grateful for is
_____.

5.
Someone I am grateful for at school is _____.

9.
I am **getting better** at
_____.

13.
My favorite **smell** is
_____.

17.
I **feel my best** when I
_____.

2. _____ and _____ make me feel **cozy.**	**3.** I get **so happy** when I see _____.	**4.** The **best part** of my day today was _____.
6. My **favorite subject** to study is _____.	**7.** I really want to **know more** about _____.	**8.** One part of my **body** that is working well is _____.
10. I am **proud** that I _____.	**11.** I love **spending** **time** with _____.	**12.** _____ makes me **laugh.**
14. My **favorite** **food** is _____.	**15.** I am **looking** **forward** to _____.	**16.** My **favorite spot** in (or outside of) my house is _____.
18. I would like to **visit** _____.	**19.** My favorite **family** **tradition** is _____.	**20.** Something I love about this **season** is _____.

We asked **National Geographic Kids** readers what they were **THANKFUL FOR**, and here are just a **few** of the many responses:

"I am thankful that people are aware of global warming and endangered animals, and want to do something about it."

"I'm thankful for clean water, because I know others don't always have it."

"I am thankful to live in a country that supports different views and opinions and gives the people a voice."

"FOOOOOODDD!"

247

WAYS TO BE THANKFUL

Give it up for all the great things in your life! There's so much to appreciate and celebrate. Check out this list of 100 ways you can put thankfulness into practice. Which one do you like doing the most? Can you think of any others?

1. Make time for belly laughs.
2. Keep a gratitude journal.
3. Use your imagination.
4. Appreciate all the amazing things your body can do.
5. Take care of your body.
6. Do what you can to make the world a better place.
7. Take good care of your pets!
8. Show your family you love them.
9. Take stock of what you do have.
10. Have a party for pizza!
11. Pay attention to your breath.
12. Be aware of your impact on the planet.
13. Love something? Learn more about its history.
14. Honor your wild ideas.
15. Take pleasure in little things.
16. Marvel at rainbows.
17. Treasure friends who just get you.
18. And treasure friends who challenge you.
19. Thank your lucky stars for cute things.
20. Jump at the chance to travel.
21. Curb the complaining.
22. Thank someone from your past.
23. Think of something you're looking forward to.
24. Turn up the music!
25. Be still.
26. Think about the best part of your day. Then share it with your family.
27. Marvel at science.
28. Follow your curiosity.
29. Learn to savor.
30. Make a gratitude pledge.
31. Get cozy.
32. Smile.
33. Treasure awesome teachers.
34. Go on adventures.
35. Celebrate all the ways you're unique!
36. Look up and admire the sky.
37. Find fun in not-so-fun tasks.
38. Introduce yourself to new kids at school.
39. Tune in to your senses.
40. Make the most of this moment.
41. Practice random acts of kindness.
42. Say "Hello" and "Goodbye."
43. Do a victory dance!
44. Make the most of your weekends.

45. Stop and smell the roses, and the cookies, and the fresh-cut grass.
46. Love.
47. Cherish the changing of the seasons.
48. Make a gratitude jar.
49. Get out into nature.
50. Take care of your things.
51. Practice mindfulness.
52. Rejoice in snow days!
53. Catch (and release) fireflies.
54. Play.
55. Embrace boredom.
56. Look in the mirror and find something you like.
57. Sit down for breakfast.
58. Treasure the stories your family tells again and again.
59. Be part of the solution.
60. Be a bookworm.
61. Learn more about your family's history.
62. Look for a lesson in struggles.
63. Celebrate today.
64. And celebrate that tomorrow is a new day.
65. Bask in bubble baths.
66. Be a wild animal advocate.
67. Always say "Thank you."
68. Write a fan letter.
69. Savor a scoop (or two or three) of ice cream.
70. Learn more about other people and celebrate what makes us different and the same.
71. Get to know your unique point of view.
72. And get to know the unique point of view of others.
73. Get lost in space.
74. Volunteer.
75. Train yourself to see beauty everywhere.
76. Be amazed by your brain (and your ability to change it).
77. Find awesome role models.
78. Admire art.
79. Be a good listener.
80. Try your best not to waste.
81. Celebrate sunshine.
82. And revel in the rain.
83. Make someone a homemade gift.
84. Speak up for those in need.
85. When you have more than you need—share.
86. Celebrate other people's achievements.
87. Seek out—then share—stuff that makes you smile.
88. Give thanks to unsung heroes! Like bees!
89. Have empathy.
90. Share your skills.
91. Celebrate everything.
92. Don't sweat the small stuff.
93. Write a good review.
94. Daydream.
95. Organize a trash cleanup.
96. Appreciate life's many surprises.
97. Be dazzled by beautiful flowers.
98. Be in awe.
99. Pay it forward.
100. Take this thankful quiz.

INDEX

Boldface indicates illustrations.
If illustrations are included within
a page span, the entire span
is **boldface**.

Find Out More

Grab a parent and visit these websites for more information!

1. natgeokids.com
2. HispanicFederation.org
3. HeForShe.org
4. LeBronJamesFamilyFoundation.org
5. Malala.org

PHOTO CREDITS

Cover and spine (kitten), Alena Ozerova/Shutterstock; cover (girl), Tom Merton/OJO Images RF/Getty Images; (rainbow), Rena Schild/Shutterstock; (headphones), Maximus256/Shutterstock; (airplane), Sakarin Sawasdina/Shutterstock; (roses), Chursina Viktorii/Shutterstock; (puppy), gillmar/Shutterstock; (boys), Sue Barr/Image Source/Getty Images; back cover, Hannamariah/Shutterstock; 1, Eric Isselee/Shutterstock; 2 (UP LE), Maximus256/Shutterstock; 2 (UP RT), James Brey/Getty Images; 2 (CTR), Art_Rich/Shutterstock; 2-3 (LO), Picsfive/Shutterstock; 3 (UP LE), Tom Merton/Getty Images; 3 (UP RT), Pticelov/Shutterstock; 3 (UP CTR), Reika/Shutterstock; 3 (LO LE), Erik Lam/Shutterstock; 5, Pflorendo/Getty; 6-7, James Pintar/Shutterstock; 7 (UP), Stockphoto Mania/Shutterstock; 7 (LO), Anan Kaewkhammu/Shutterstock; 7 (sweatband on tiger), T_Kimura/Getty; 8-9, Um-Umm/Shutterstock; 8-11 (doodles), Mhatzapa/Shutterstock; 10-11, Billion Photos/Shutterstock; 12-13, Sergey Nivens/Shutterstock; 12 (UFO), Koya979/Shutterstock; 15, Sergey Novikov/Shutterstock; 16, Kazoka/Shutterstock; 18 (LE), Mike Windle/Getty Images; 18 (mittens), Rusian Kudrin/Shutterstock; 19 (UP), Karkas/Shutterstock; 19 (snowflake), Anfisa Focusova/Shutterstock; 20 (UP), Nikolai Sorokin/Dreamstime; 20 (LO LE), Terrace Studio/Shutterstock; 20 (LO RT), Andrey Armyagov/Shutterstock; 21 (UP), Rusian Kudrin/Shutterstock; 21 (LO), Andrey Armyagov/Shutterstock; 22, Prpunn/Shutterstock; 23, Food.kiro/Shutterstock; 24-25, Matthew Rakola; 27, Rich Vintage/Getty Images; 28, Topseller/Shutterstock; 29, Best Photo Studio/Shutterstock; 30, Olegganko/Shutterstock; 31 (pepperoni), Binh Thanh Bui/Shutterstock; 31 (party hat), Macrovector/Shutterstock; 31 (pizza), Seregam/Shutterstock; 31 (confetti), Shutterstock; 32, John T Takai/Shutterstock; 33, XiXinXing/Getty Images; 34-35, Fizkes/Shutterstock; 35, John T Takai/Shutterstock; 36-39, Vlad61/Shutterstock; 39 (UP), Allegra Boverman MIT News/National Geographic Creative; 39 (LO), Stuart Armstrong; 40-41 (BACKGROUND), Neuevector/Shutterstock; 40, James Brey/Getty Images; 41, Bettmann/Getty Images; 42-43, Jeffrey Coolidge/Getty Images; 44, Bildagentur Zoonar GmbH/Shutterstock; 45 (girl), PERO Studio/Shutterstock; 45 (orange), Reika/Shutterstock; 45 (bubble wrap), Alex Alekseev/Shutterstock; 46-47, Svetlana57/Alamy; 47, Pticelov/Shutterstock; 49, Iordani/Shutterstock; 50-51, Light Field Studios/Shutterstock; 52, Jagodka/Shutterstock; 53, Eric Isselee/Shutterstock; 54, Erika Skogg; 55, Vadim Georgiev/Shutterstock; 56, Hakinmhan/Shutterstock; 56-57, Erika Skogg; 59, Khabarushka/Shutterstock; 60-61, Flipser/Shutterstock; 60-61 (stamps), Flipser/Shutterstock; 61 (envelope), Veniamin Kraskov/Shutterstock; 61 (hand), Natthi Phaocharoen/Shutterstock; 62-63, 5 Second Studio/Shutterstock; 64, Yulia Lavrova/Shutterstock; 65, Sonsedska/iStockphoto/Getty Images; 66-67, Chuanpis/Shutterstock; 68-69, Willee Cole Phototgraphy/Shutterstock; 70-71, NotarYes/Shutterstock; 71, Hurst Photo/Shutterstock; 72, Sasha Haltam/Shutterstock; 74 (UP), Adriatic Foto/Shutterstock; 74 (LO), BeRad/Shutterstock; 75, George Rudy/Shutterstock; 76-77, Sirtravelalot/Shutterstock; 76-77 (doodles), Mhatzapa/Shutterstock; 78-79, Stas Knop/Shutterstock; 80-81, Redpixel.Pl/Shutterstock; 83, Wave Break Media/Shutterstock; 84-84, Elena Elisseeva/Shutterstock; 85, Yuyula/Shutterstock; 86, Kalamurzing/Shutterstock; 87, Koltukovs/Shutterstock; 88-89, Kisialiou Yury/Shutterstock; 90-93, Chris Johns; 94-95, Eric Isselee/Shutterstock; 94-95 (BACKGROUND), I.H. Liu/Shutterstock; 97, VVita/Shutterstock; 98-99, Exopixel/Shutterstock; 100-101, Monkey Business Images/Shutterstock; 102-103, Pap Kutasi Szilvia/Shutterstock; 104, Sinelev/Shutterstock; 105 (pottery), George Nazmi Bebawi/Shutterstock; 105 (reading), Kim Songsak/Shutterstock; 107, Quinn Martin/Shutterstock; 107 (LO), Olga Kovalenko/Shutterstock; 108, Mahathir Mohd Yasin/Shutterstock; 109 (UP), Yellowj/Shutterstock; 109 (LO), Javier Brosch/Shutterstock; 110-111, Lemon Tree Images/Shutterstock; 112-113 (BACKGROUND), Markus Pfaff/Shutterstock; 113, Hajakely/Shutterstock; 114-115, Sergey Novikov/Dreamstime; 116-117, Ramon Antinolo/Shutterstock; 118, TaLaNoVa/Shutterstock; 119, Pattaya Photography/Shutterstock; 120, Elena Zajchikova/Shutterstock; 121, Sakurra/Shutterstock; 122 (UP), Eric Gevaert/Shutterstock; 122

For my best friend and sister, Alison, for
who I am so very thankful. —L.M.G.

Since 1888, the National Geographic Society has funded more
than 12,000 research, exploration, and preservation projects
around the world. The Society receives funds from National
Geographic Partners, LLC, funded in part by your purchase.
A portion of the proceeds from this book supports this vital
work. To learn more, visit natgeo.com/info.

For more information, visit nationalgeographic.com, call
1-800-647-5463, or write to the following address:

National Geographic Partners
1145 17th Street N.W.
Washington, D.C. 20036-4688 U.S.A.

Visit us online at nationalgeographic.com/books

For librarians and teachers: ngchildrensbooks.org

More for kids from National Geographic: natgeokids.com

National Geographic Kids magazine inspires children to explore
their world with fun yet educational articles on animals, science, nature, and more. Using fresh storytelling and amazing
photography, *Nat Geo Kids* shows kids ages 6 to 14 the fascinating truth about the world—and why they should care.
kids.nationalgeographic.com/subscribe

For information about special discounts for bulk purchases,
please contact National Geographic Books Special Sales:
specialsales@natgeo.com

For rights or permissions inquiries, please contact
National Geographic Books Subsidiary Rights:
bookrights@natgeo.com

Designed by Rose Gowsell-Pattison

The publisher would like to thank the team who helped make
this book possible: Ariane Szu-Tu, editor; Lori Epstein, photo
director; Callie Broaddus, art director; Molly Reid, production
editor; and Gus Tello and Anne LeongSon, design production
assistants.

Library of Congress Cataloging-in-Publication Data
Names: Gerry, Lisa, author.
Title: 100 ways to be thankful / Lisa M. Gerry.
Other titles: One hundred ways to be thankful
Description: Washington, DC : National Geographic Kids, 2019.
| Audience: Age: 8-12. | Audience: Grade 4 to 6.
Identifiers: LCCN 2018036047| ISBN 9781426332753
  (paperback) | ISBN 9781426332760 (hardcover)
Subjects: LCSH: Gratitude--Juvenile literature. | BISAC:
  JUVENILE NONFICTION / Social Issues / Values & Virtues. |
  JUVENILE NONFICTION / Social Issues / Manners &
  Etiquette. | JUVENILE NONFICTION / Body, Mind & Spirit.
Classification: LCC BF575.G68 G47 2019 | DDC 179.9--dc23
LC record available at https://lccn.loc.gov/2018036047

Printed in China
18/PPS/1